MY PINK CANE AND ME

6-Time, Stage 4, Aggressive Metastatic
Ovarian Cancer Survivor's Journey

Nora Bautista Gorman

Dedication

I dedicate this book to all of the people who helped me through this tumultuous journey. For all of their prayers, kindness, care, and understanding. For the rides to appointments, trips to the grocery store, free delicious meals, encouraging words, cards/gifts, and listening ears. I have so much love and appreciation for all of you. And, I am forever grateful for everything you have done for both Megan and me!

To my beautiful, caring, and kind daughter Megan whose selfless act of putting her life on hold to take care of me during my battle with cancer, surgeries, treatments, and side effects, truly helped me tremendously. Words are not enough to express how proud, appreciative, thankful, and grateful I am of her.

To my ultimate, kind, incredibly generous, compassionate, beautiful, and loyal best friend Beth, her supportive and unbelievable good sense of humor husband Kress, and their beautiful and smart kids Ryan, Kendall, and Matt (Kress, Jr.) Her thoughtful and wonderful parents Geri and Norm for all the prayers and for always being there for me and Megan before, during, and after cancer. I call them my chosen loving and caring family. I am actually closer to them than almost all of my blood relatives combined. I have many blood relatives too, so that says a lot about them!

To my brother Rico who died unexpectedly just a few hours ago while I was writing this section. He fought for his life until the end but suffered a lot in the process. I find comfort in knowing that he is no longer suffering, but very sad that I will not be able to talk to him anymore. Until we see each other again. Rest easy my protector, caring, and loving brother. Love you so much and please say hi to mom, dad, and sister Tess.

To my loving, amazing, and caring sister Lynne who's always been there for me in prayers, long phone conversations, laughter, just shooting the breeze, being emotional, and everything. Lynne is one of my prayer warriors. Tess and Rico were my prayer warriors too but they both died unexpectedly during my cancer journey. Her husband Rolly and her thoughtful children Rafael, and Shelly as well.

To my kind, caring, gorgeous, and loving then 17 years old now 19 years old niece Kendall who baked and gave away free dozens and dozens of delicious high-end cupcakes to the compassionate and stressed-out frontliners, first responders, and staff at my favorite hospital, Edward-Elmhurst hospital, Cancer Center, Roselle Police Department and two Fire Departments (Roselle and Lisle) during the unforgettable 2020 COVID-19 pandemic.

To my thoughtful, kind-natured mentor and good friend Gwen Henry, who is also a breast cancer survivor for taking time out of her extremely busy schedule to check up on me from time to time.

To my ex-husband and Megan's dad, Jim for helping Megan and me during those uncertain years.

To Kelly Gorman. Megan's cousin, who drove us to one of my surgeries, waited at the hospital with Megan until my surgery was over and picked up my prescription.

To my good friends Luz and Gloria for always being there for Megan and me and always ready to give me a ride wherever I needed to go. And, those spontaneous lunch get-togethers are very much appreciated.

To the two compassionate and wonderful people I met at Edward-Elmhurst Hospital Cancer Center and who later became my true friends. Sharon (retired social worker) and Kimmie (former front desk staff). I miss both their listening ears and moral support at the Cancer Center.

To my first cousins, Evelyn who offered to pay for my round-trip tickets to the Philippines to give me a break from cancer (which I respectfully and politely declined), thank you, though!

Aurora, nana Concha (deceased), and my nieces Marnie and Shannon for the hospital and home visits, free lunches, dinners, and for praying for me to get better. I appreciate you all.

To my first cousins Tina, Maris, Lolly, Rick, Gee, Juliet, uncle Oscar, and nana Nene (deceased) for all the prayers and for organizing and hosting our family reunion before my first cancer.

To my uncle Dr. Dan, auntie Letty, auntie Ofelia, uncle Zoilo, auntie Zeny, auntie Perlita, Deidre, Gen, Jordan and Dr. Germaine for all the prayers and moral support.

To my fellow cancer survivors and friends that I met at my hospital: Wendy and Terri who visited me at the Cancer Center during one of my chemotherapy treatments. Megan and I appreciated that a lot. Harold, Leslie, Jean, Diane, and Bessma, including our friend Lynn who didn't make it.

To Rasa, my hairstylist who cut my hair really short before it started falling out during rounds of chemotherapy, not knowing that she is a cancer survivor herself. I still go to her for haircuts and I consider her one of my good friends.

To Dr. Edyta Straczynski (my kind, thorough, and newest primary doctor). She is also a breast cancer survivor. So she personally knew and experienced what I went through. Her nice and friendly nurses Robinn and Ava.

To my trusted, faithful, and loyal high school best friend Ruby and her daughter Ana Marie for their prayers and moral support. Also to our high school classmate and friend Grace for her prayers and moral support as well.

To all my family and friends Mella, Almira, Cassie, Ress, Mark, Carla, JM, Salve, Lito, Paolo, Rael, Jhen, Angel, Frank, Terri, Mariel, Dr. Sonia, Lorna, Teya, Bong, Jojo, Candice, Nneka, Denden, Noreen (breast cancer survivor), Nick, Uncle Pablo, Dr. Iris, Dr. Jerica, Dr. Duane, Dr. Faith, Dr. Dyan, Lilibeth, Ayds, Flor (first cousin breast cancer survivor), Dr. Emilyn, Rowena, Dr. Edith, tita Baby, Vangie, Thelma, Arlene, Rochelle, Gerlie, Vicky, Tammy, Fawzia, Madeleine, Danny, Britt, Brooke, Toni, Edith B, Nard, Irah, Ching, Vic, Lulu (deceased), Wendy H, Joey, Roann, Char (fellow cancer survivor), Robyn and all the kind, compassionate and wonderful people who crossed my path the last 11 years of my life and prayed for me to get better.

To my thoughtful and close friend Sue. We are both obsessed with cardinals and we believe that when you see a cardinal bird in your yard, your loved one is visiting. Which is something that has helped both of us during very difficult times.

To all the cancer patients, cancer survivors, those who are battling other deadly diseases, to those who didn't make it, especially my first cousins Ellen and Daisy who died of colon cancer and breast cancer at a very young age respectively, my uncles Jose, Hermie, Romy and Junior who died of the throat, colon, lung and liver cancer, their friends and family and to all the caregivers for their kindness, love, caring, and understanding and who gave up so much to take care of others. My hat's off to all the caregivers!

To all my doctors, especially Dr. Alex Hantel, MD, Oncologist, my oncologist for the last 12 years. He will be retiring in April 2023. Nurse Maria, his medical team, nurses, technicians, and staff at the Cancer Center of Edward-Elmhurst Hospital for their kind and compassionate work to keep me alive.

To all my friends and family who encouraged me to put my cancer journey story in writing. Isn't it obvious that I listened to you?

To all my readers. May you stay healthy, and safe and learn something from my own cancer journey. Hopefully, you will be able to discuss my story with your friends and family to be inspired and give them hope.

To Pat, Wally, Steve, and Connor for helping us out with work inside and outside the house for many years even before, during, and after my cancer. Sami, my hard working high school neighbor is now helping us mow the lawn. I am certainly blessed and proud to call all of them my wonderful friends.

To my loyal, supportive college best friends, Tina, Ada, Sandra, Espy, Angela, Eva (breast cancer survivor), Alice, Rose, Chato, and Chabs, and to our dear friend, Frocie who lost her life to colon cancer at the young age of 48 years old.

To my long-time California and Oregon good friends Shannon, Jo, Bridget, JoAnn, Jessica, and the rest of the Murphy family for their friendship over the years, prayers, and moral support.

To the only person who has known me the longest other than my own family, my elementary school classmate, and friend, Beth, for praying for me to get better.

To my sister Tess' best friends who were with her during that final trip. Edith, Elna, Heidi, Milani, and others who stayed at the hospital with her until her own family arrived. Even though Glo wasn't there with them, she was still able to organize a blood drive to help my sister Tess with her much needed blood transfusions. I appreciate you all. Thank you.

Finally, I dedicate this book to my sister Tess, my parents Mely and Federico, Sr. for everything they have done for me and my siblings our entire lives. I miss and love you all so much! There are so many things I wanted to talk to you about but I'll wait until we all see each other again! They are all looking down on us from up in heaven. Thank you very much, everyone!

Acknowledgment:

I would like to thank my medical team (for keeping me alive), physical, eye, oral and financial team. My family and friends without whom I wouldn't have been able to write this book for people to read and learn about my cancer journey. I feel incredibly blessed! Thank you, everyone!

Dr. Alex Hantel, MD, System Medical Director, Oncology Services, Edward-Elmhurst Hospital, Cancer Center

Dr. Carol Weinberg, MD, my former primary doctor, who because of her sympathetic nature, helped discover my stage 4 aggressive metastatic ovarian cancer

Dr. Potkul, MD, Head of Ovarian Cancer Surgeon, Loyola Medical Center. Performed my ovarian cancer and hysterectomy surgeries

The American Red Cross for all the donated blood I received during my surgeries and chemotherapy treatments

The American Cancer Society called me to say that they are there if I needed anything. That meant a lot to me. And, for giving me a free wig

Dr. Neil Das Gupta, MD, Radiation Oncologist, Head Radiology Dept Edward-Elmhurst Hospital, Cancer Center for the cyber knife radiation therapy recommendation.

Dr. Heidi E. Eklund, MD, Radiologist Mammography Dept Edward-Elmhurst Hospital and staff

Edward-Elmhurst Hospital, Cancer Center staff, nurses Maria, Jill, Liz, Sue, Juliet, Stacey, Stefanie, Sherri, Head nurse Derrick (retired) receptionists Debbie, Marie, Vicki, and social worker, Sharon (retired), Kimmie (Plainfield), and others

Edward-Elmhurst Hospital Health Center Back on Track program staff, Brooke, Britt (former staff), and Toni

Dr. Chiann Fan Gibson, DMD, AAACD, Dentist-owner, Smiles by Dr. Gibson of Promenade Dental for providing me with free dental work during my cancer. Her dental staff Suzy (former employee), Daisy, Tala, and others

Dr. John Chae, DDS, Oral Surgeon, Naperville Dental Specialist

for teeth extraction and followed up with me the same night to find out if I was okay. Doctor's phone call after office hours. Impressive!

Dr. Louis Montana, MD, Integrated Oncology Program, Surgery, DuPage Medical Group

Dr. Edyta Straczynski, MD, my newest Primary Doctor, and nurses Robbinn and Ava, Edward Medical Group

Edward-Elmhurst Hospital
Physical Therapy Dept, Therapists and staff

Ms. Doreen Berard, RD, LDN, Why Weight Program, Edward-Elmhurst Hospital, Cancer Center

Ms. Susan Lewis, CPA, Susan Lewis Ltd, who compassionately didn't bill me for preparing my taxes during my cancer years and staff

Ms. Gwen Henry, CPA, Treasurer, DuPage County. My good friend and mentor who despite being extremely busy still manages to check up on me from time to time

Dr. Kimberly Garvey, Dr. Gardner, Optometrists, Audrey, Office Manager, Vision Source who made me feel safe and at ease with their covid-19 office precautions

Ms. Kristi Grimm, VP, A.W.E. Air. Water. Energy. AWE's Customer Service, Sales, Maintenance, and Installation of our new A/C and furnace are undeniably the BEST in their industry. Their honesty, professionalism, work ethic, and protocols for the pandemic are simply outstanding. Especially when I told them that I was in remission for my six cancers and I am included in the high-risk group. They wore their masks the whole time, maintained a safe distance, and always had their shoe covers on inside my house which I truly appreciated.

Ms. Marnie Reyes, AVP, Bank of America, my kind, compassionate, supportive and thoughtful niece gave me a ride to the wig-fitting place, brought us food, drove me to work and back home when I couldn't, etc.

Articles written about me and my cancer journey over the past few years to inspire and give hope to others. They are from our local newspaper (Naperville Patch on 01/31/2017) by Edward-Elmhurst Health - Community Contributor, online websites (Patch.com and glancermagazine.com), magazine (Glancer Magazine 02/01/2018 edition) by Mindy Kyle, and the short version of my cancer story can be found on the Edward-Elmhurst Hospital's website: www.eehealth.org/about-us/community-benefit written by Keith Hartenberger and photos by Robyn Sheldon.

Thank you, everyone!

Special Thank You:

Ms. Beth Stein, President, Maze Graphic Design https://www.mazegraphicdesign.com/ My best friend, Beth created, painted, and designed this amazing book cover for free while spending Spring break with her college daughters in Arizona. That was the only free time she had from her extremely hectic work schedule. She's such a dedicated and loyal best friend that I am very blessed and lucky to have. I love and appreciate you and your work very much. Thanks a million!

CONTENTS

INTRODUCTION:

Hello everyone, my name is Nora Bautista Gorman. I am not a professional writer or any writer for that matter. To be absolutely honest, this is the first and the last book that I will ever write in my entire life. I made a living as an accountant and a banker for well over 40 years. I really enjoyed doing that. But I had a forced retirement due to stage 4 aggressive metastatic ovarian cancer and chemotherapy side effects. I am now a 6-time cancer survivor!

After 11 years of contemplating whether I should write a book about my cancer journey or not, I finally made the decision to put in writing all the things, good and bad, that I have experienced during this time of my life. My story in this book is raw, emotional, unexpected, and encouraging. I wanted to write this book to inspire and give hope to cancer patients who are currently battling this awful disease. These are my words and this is my story.

I learned a lot during those uncertain and challenging years. Although I was born and raised Catholic and even graduated from the oldest Catholic University in Asia, I have not been to church in a very long time for personal reasons which I will not discuss here. I learned to pray more with all my heart now. I pray the rosary five times a day.

I also learned to appreciate things that did not matter

to me before cancer. I learned to care for others more this time. I don't really care for material things anymore for myself, but I feel wonderful when I give them to others. I now also understand the true meaning of love, compassion, kindness, support, and care from my friends and family and in some cases from strangers, too.

I learned that it is perfectly alright to accept help from others as well. I must admit that this is something I had difficulty accepting before cancer. Because I always saw and considered myself as the giver and not the taker.

When I help others, I really don't expect anything in return. I just want to help others who are a little less fortunate than myself. In one of my conversations with Sharon, one of the cancer center's social workers, I mentioned that I feel guilty accepting help from others.

She then asked me how I felt when I was helping others. I said that I always feel great. Well then, the kind and wonderful people who are helping you now feel the same way, she responded.

I think that's all I needed to hear from someone other than my daughter Megan to accept help from others. Sometimes you are up and sometimes you are down. There's no shame in being down and there's no shame in admitting that and accepting help.

I can vividly remember this super kind lady named Char who worked at a nearby gas station. She rushed to the door to help me open it when she saw me struggling to open the door. It was just a few days after one of my surgeries.

I was on my way home from work when I decided to fill up

the car. So I didn't have to do it before work the following morning. She actually became one of my friends since then. I later found out that she herself is a breast cancer survivor too.

Also, I am not too proud to admit that Medicaid Insurance helped me a few times during my cancer years as well because I couldn't afford to pay for my health insurance anymore.

And, I will never ever forget that I was helped by the kindness and generosity of Edward-Elmhurst Hospital's Charity Foundation with my hospital bills for a few years. Whatever my Medicare health insurance did not cover, the hospital covered. So, I didn't have to worry about my hospital bills piling up. That was a huge help for me and others who are going through cancer. The cost of cancer treatments is astronomical.

Instead, it allowed me to concentrate on getting better and healthier. I am forever grateful, thankful, and appreciative! What truly matters to me now are staying healthy, enjoying life to the fullest with my daughter Megan, friends, and family, living longer, and paying it forward by continuing to help others as I can.

> *I live by the mantra that "early detection is the only key to cancer survival". My advice to all of you is to go for your regular blood tests, mammograms and colonoscopy. It might just save your own life too like it did mine!*

I have included all the side effects of chemotherapy that I experienced in this book, many of which just plain stunk.

But, the honest truth is that I would not have been able to write this book for you to read and learn from my experience if not for the chemotherapy treatments.

Despite all the side effects, the 36 rounds of chemotherapy treatments that I underwent, including 14 days of oral chemotherapy, worked for me.

It did its job and killed my stage 4 aggressive metastatic ovarian cancer. The side effects of chemotherapy are different for different cancer patients and it can be very scary. Please listen to your oncologist's recommendation regarding treatments. The doctors truly do know best!

I had a friend who died of breast cancer because she did not listen to her oncologist. She heard stories about the side effects of chemotherapy and she did not want to go through with it. Instead, she went for other natural medicines, which did not get rid of her cancer.

When she finally decided to have breast surgery and chemotherapy treatments, it was a little too late. Her breast cancer already spread to different parts of her vital organs like her lungs, liver, and bones.

And surgery and chemotherapy were out of the question at that point. Within just a few months, she passed away. Her story was not the first one I heard about or the last.

I highly recommend chemotherapy treatments to all the people who are fighting cancer right now. What have you got to lose at this point? You need to have faith in your doctors and the process.

As the patient, you will always have the final say in what your treatments will be, but you also have to trust your doctor's expertise.

Chemotherapy can be awful, but, as of right now, it is our best way to fight this terrible disease. Maybe, just maybe, chemotherapy will work for you, too? Good Luck to all of you! You are all included in my daily prayers.

Let us all remember that stage 4 cancer is not always a "death sentence". I am just one living proof among thousands of cancer survivors! Never ever lose hope. Thank you, GOD!!!

CHAPTER 1: THIS IS MY STORY...

L ike I said in my intro, I wrote this book to inspire and give hope to more people who are currently battling cancer, cancer survivors, caregivers, friends, and family who are going through cancer with their loved ones. I always believe that it is the journey that inspires people and not the destination!

I have been a 6-time stage 4 aggressive metastatic ovarian cancer survivor for more than six years now. My first cancer (right breast cancer) stage 0 started in October 2010, my second cancer was stage 4 aggressive metastatic ovarian cancer in November 2011, my third cancer left breast stage 0 in 2013, my fourth cancer right neck lymph nodes stage 4 in November 2014, fifth cancer left side next to my rib cage stage 4 in late 2015, and my last cancer right side above my shoulder blade stage 4 was in February 2016. I haven't had any additional cancer since June 2016 when I had my last chemotherapy treatments. I was officially declared in remission in October 2021 by my oncologist, Dr. Hantel, MD. Thank you so much, GOD! Thank you so much, Dr. Hantel, MD

Articles have been written about my cancer journey via local newspaper (Naperville Patch on 01/31/2017), online websites (Patch.com and glancermagazine.com), magazine (Glancer

Magazine 02/01/2018 edition), and the short version of my cancer story can be found on the Edward-Elmhurst Hospital's website: www.eehealth.org/about-us/community-benefit to inspire and give hope to others.

It is worth mentioning that I was one of the case studies of the intelligent minds at the Edward-Elmhurst Hospital in Naperville, IL. This group consists of doctors, oncologists, surgeons, nurses and medical staff. They meet once a week. I was told that to avoid being biased, they do not have names of the cancer patients only case study numbers. I was part of their case study more than once. I guess to find out why I am still alive?

It is important to note that my compassionate, kind, and caring daughter Megan was my sole caregiver. She put her life on hold for at least 6 years to take care of me all throughout my cancer journey. Some days I felt like she had sacrificed and suffered more than I did because she personally saw what I went through.

I know it has been very difficult for her to see me suffering like that. The first six years of my cancer were the toughest because it seemed like there was no end to my cancer, surgeries, treatments, and side effects.

At the end of the seventh year, in 2017, I started telling Megan that it is time to take care of herself now and not to worry about me anymore. I pray every day that she doesn't get cancer and go through what I went through!

Between the years 2017 - 2021, I finally received a respite and I did not have to deal with another cancer, surgeries, chemotherapy treatments, and side effects. I am praying and hoping that it will continue for many more years to come.

Although I am still being checked for my ovarian cancer level, blood tests, other procedures, and follow-up with my oncologist, Dr. Hantel, MD on a regular basis, it is nothing compared to what I went through with cancer, surgeries, treatments, and the side effects for the first six years.

This book is a raw (I did not sugarcoat anything) and detailed experience of my physical, mental, spiritual, financial, and emotional pain, sacrifices, and sufferings that I went through battling cancer, surgeries, chemotherapy, regular radiation, cyberknife radiation, and all the side effects. Unfortunately, it has been over eleven years now since my very first cancer and I am still going through lymphedema and some of the side effects of chemotherapy, etc and I suppose I will be for the rest of my life.

I now have chemo brain, neuropathy in both my hands and feet (the reason why I walk with my pink cane since 2016), eczema below my eyebrows and outside both of my ears, my eyelashes and eyebrows never grew back, lymphedema in my right arm, and my ROM (range of motion) is not 100% anymore because of lymph nodes removed in my right armpit. But, I shouldn't really complain. After all, chemotherapy treatments are one of the reasons why I am still alive.

While I was being treated for my stage 4 aggressive metastatic ovarian cancer, my oncologist, Dr. Hantel, MD recommended that I take a genetic test which I did. It's a blood test to determine if my cancer is hereditary or environmental. My blood sample was sent to a laboratory in Utah. One of the very few laboratories that specialized in genetic testing during that time.

After a few days, a simple blood test showed that I tested positive for the BRCA 2 gene and according to my oncologist, BRCA2 positive patients respond very well to chemotherapy in comparison to BRCA1 positive patients. Per CDC.gov, the simple explanation for BRCA1 and BRCA2 are two genes that are important to fighting cancer. They are tumor suppressor genes. When they work normally, these genes help keep breast, ovarian and other types of cells from growing and dividing too rapidly or in an uncontrolled way.

Dr. Hantel said they are finding out that it is like a double-edged sword. I have cancer but because of my BRCA2 positive gene, that same gene is also fighting the cancer itself. In some cases, it is killing the actual cancer. I pray and hope that it is killing my own cancer. This is another blessing that I am BRCA2 positive. Thank GOD again! Also, my cancer is hereditary and not environmental per the genetic test results.

I am now absolutely certain that my cancer is from my father's side of the family, not necessarily my father because my father died of a heart attack and stroke at a very young age of fifty years old.

I had four uncles Jose, Hermie, Romy and Junior who died of throat, colon, lung and liver cancer, and two first cousins Ellen and Daisy who died of colon and breast cancer respectively.

And, no one had cancer or died of cancer on my mother's side of the family that I am aware of. I am also definitely sure that my mother's oncologist in California was accurate in his diagnosis that my mother never had cancer. But she still underwent chemotherapy and cobalt radiation treatments and all the side effects that she did not need but ordered by her greedy, dishonest and power hungry doctor/oncologist in the Philippines.

That Filipino doctor diagnosed my mom with throat cancer that apparently showed in the right side of her neck. My mom never had another blood test and other procedure other than what that doctor did.

When we suggested to him that our mom needed a second opinion, he flatly said no need. He is the best doctor/oncologist around. How can we disagree with that? He was so confident in saying that he was the best. But that was a big lie and an absolute mistake on my mother's and our part.

Come to think of it now, after my mom's suffering, we should have insisted on another doctor's opinion. We should not have been intimidated by that SOB Filipino doctor but we all did. I must admit that was a terrible lesson learned but very helpful.

I actually started writing this book a few years ago, but ended up losing the pages, so I am telling my story starting from scratch now. This is no easy task with my chemo brain (another lovely side effect). But, I will try my very best to remember almost everything that happened to me accurately for the last eleven years. Some of the dates might be off a little bit but the years I can certainly attest to and vividly remember! So, here it goes!

CHAPTER 2: IT IS CANCER

My journey began in October 2010. I went in for my routine mammogram and Dexa bone density exams, etc. before I went on a long weekend trip to Las Vegas and California with my older sister Tess. I flew in from Illinois to Las Vegas and Tess flew in from the Philippines to Las Vegas.

We met at the airport and from there we went straight to our hotel. Tess and I stayed in Las Vegas for two days. We had dinner that night with our first cousins Maris and Rick. We gambled a little bit and met some friends Joey and his wife Roann the following day. They made a delicious dinner for us and drove us around the Vegas Strip. We then went inside different hotels to take pictures and post on social media. We took so many pictures that we really had a hard time choosing which ones to post. That was really fun!

It was at a hotel in Las Vegas where Tess and I stayed when I received a phone call from my doctor's office that I needed to redo my mammogram because they found some suspicious abnormalities in my right breast. The news was definitely alarming and concerning but, I put it behind me and proceeded to fly to California with Tess from Las Vegas. We enjoyed our visit with our family and friends. I was elated to see my relatives and friends in Las Vegas and southern California that I have not seen in many years.

Tess traveled a lot when she was still alive so she saw them at least every two years. We stayed at my first cousin's Tina's house the first and second nights in California and stayed at my sister Tess' best friend's Edith's house the third night. It was Edith and her husband Nard who gave me a ride to the airport the following morning. They were all so welcoming and accomodating.

We surely enjoyed each other's company. Old and new stories were told, I met their children, spouses and in-laws, the abundance of delicious food, drinks were certainly flowing and just being with each other for the long weekend was an absolute treat that we will not soon forget. Thank you very much to my first cousins Tina (sons William and Chris), Maris, Lolly, Rick, uncle Oscar and aunt Nene (deceased) and their family for coordinating and hosting this enjoyable, unforgettable and wonderful pool-side family reunion in Tina's gorgeous home. My oldest first cousin, Frank and his wife, Terry were there, my first cousin, Ayds and her son, Karlo were there too as well as many of our relatives and friends Edith, Ching, Nards, Vic, Lulu (deceased).

The rest of the guests, I don't remember their names. Sorry, it's not intentional, it's my chemo brain. We promised each other to have another reunion sooner than later. Little did I know that that was the last time I would ever travel outside of my home state, Illinois. That was eleven years ago.

I remember fearing that I might have breast cancer at the airport coming back home from California but I didn't tell anyone including my sister Tess who stayed longer in California to spend more time with her long time best friends Edith, Ching, Lulu (deceased), of what I was thinking because I didn't want her and them to worry. I have always told my daughter Megan that worrying will never change the outcome! And, this was no different.

My four hour flight from California to Illinois certainly gave me a lot of time to think of the woulda, coulda, shoulda scenarios of having breast cancer. What should I do if I have breast cancer and will I survive it? I was more worried about my daughter Megan because she is my only child.

At this point I was blaming myself for not having another child. I was thinking if I had two children then Megan would not be alone when I die. At least she'll have a brother or a sister to cope up with when I am already gone. The big unknown of my future and Megan's was surely evident! But during this flight thinking and praying was all I could do. I had no idea what was ahead of me.

As soon as I got back to Illinois, I scheduled my second mammogram. I am the type of person who normally doesn't get nervous about almost anything. But this situation was different. I was getting a little nervous. This time my daughter Megan was with me for moral and emotional support. Having a mammogram on both breasts again within less than a couple of weeks apart was very painful. But the doctor informed me that I needed to have another mammogram to make sure that there was no error on the results of the first mammogram. So, I did. Well, the result was the same as the first one. There were abnormal cells growing in my right breast.

So, after the mammogram, I had an ultrasound. Then, I had an MRI on both breasts and needle biopsy on my right breast. It was one of the most painful procedures I have been through up until that point. Little did I know that there would be more painful and eventful procedures coming all throughout my cancer journey. After I was done with all the procedures, I was taken to another room by a person who was in charge of finding out about my insurance coverage.

As soon as I got back to work from my vacation, I informed my former boss that I was leaving my job to focus on my accounting business. I handed her my letter of resignation and gave her two months to find my replacement. Talking about perfect timing, huh? Now, I will be out of insurance since I would continue working as an independent contractor.

I informed the insurance person of this and she suggested that I purchase cobra insurance once my work insurance expires. I did, but I wasn't even remotely aware that it would cost me over $700.00 a month for 18 months out of pocket just for myself! But, it was the best decision I made considering the health issues that I would soon face.

Meanwhile, my daughter Megan had been in the waiting room for hours when she actually overheard my doctor/surgeon and a nurse talking to each other with the door open about the fact that I had breast cancer. They didn't name any names, but they talked about the timing of me leaving my job.

So, as much as she didn't want to believe that they were talking about me, what were the odds that it was about someone else? Of course they didn't realize that my daughter could hear their conversation from where she was seated nor was she trying to listen to them. However, because of that, my daughter knew that I had breast cancer before I actually knew it.

She didn't have the benefit of being informed gently about it either, like most patients & the families, do. Megan found out via a matter-of-fact routine diagnosis conversation between a doctor/surgeon and a nurse. She was terrified, but she also still tried to hold on to the small hope that it wasn't me that they were talking about or that they were wrong.

After all the procedures were done and consultation with my doctor/surgeon, we were sent home. To be perfectly honest, I did not feel my feet walking to the elevator and parking lot. I just felt completely numb! I could not believe what I just heard. The doctor told me that she believed that I had right breast cancer and I needed a lumpectomy as soon as possible to find out if it really was breast cancer and what stage it was. I have heard of the word lumpectomy before but I didn't know what lumpectomy surgery really means until my doctor/surgeon's explanation. It needed to be done right away too.

Megan and I did not talk on our way to the car. We were both quiet and kept walking. We both did not expect what we just heard. In the car, Megan told me what she overheard and kept telling me I had right breast cancer.

Here, I was trying to be strong and not cry because I did not want her to worry and cry either. I tried to tell her that it was in a very early stage and the doctor/surgeon will be able to remove the cancer completely if it was indeed cancer.

Before leaving my doctor/surgeon's office, I was scheduled for a lumpectomy in my right breast at Edward-Elmhurst Hospital which is just a few minutes away from my house. I just kept praying that I was right, I will be alright and Megan will be fine too! Afterall, early detection is the only key to cancer survival! I just hoped that they had found it early enough.

The only problem was I just had to convince and believe in what I was telling myself and Megan. I have been known to always be positive and determined. Annoyingly positive at times, to be blunt. I believe and always have strong faith in GOD! So, at that moment, I felt like I was really being tested.

My First Right Breast Lumpectomy

My first right breast lumpectomy surgery was in November 2010 the week before Thanksgiving. When the doctors say breast lumpectomy surgery, it does not really mean you will be on the operating table right away.

There is a procedure that they have to follow and do first which I was not aware of or maybe they told me I just was not paying attention. They had me sign all the standard hospital waivers documents. You know the documents that if something goes wrong with the patient during surgery? The hospital, doctors, nurses and medical staff are not liable? Yeah, that one!

One of the procedures I think was the sentinel node biopsy before the surgery. It is a long needle that was inserted in my right breast. I knew there was anesthetic used to numb my right breast but I felt every centimeter of that long needle inside my right breast.

I was in terrible pain and literally fell on my knees and one of the nurses, nurse Jill was able to hold and pull me back up. Tears rolled down my face and I was really scared at that instance that I started praying for GOD to be with me and take care of my daughter if I don't make it out of the operating room alive.

Little did I know that was the first surgery of many more surgeries to come all throughout my cancer years. There was another procedure done before they wheeled me in the operating table but I could not remember the name of it.

I believe the surgeon left color coded clips in my right breast to identify where the cancer was. At this point my right breast because of so many mammograms, MRI, needle biopsy, lumpectomy surgery, etc my right breast was now in full trauma.

This lumpectomy surgery procedure was an out of patient surgery. My daughter Megan was waiting for me in the recovery room. We were sent home after I felt better to go home.

Although I was not supposed to take a shower until the following day, I could not lay in my own bed without taking a shower and washing my hair first.

So, I wrapped both my breasts with Saran Wrap so the water would not be able to penetrate through the bandages and wet my fresh surgical incision and caused an infection. I was as careful as I could be and luckily nothing bad happened to me because of that shower.

My Second Right Breast Lumpectomy

I had to have two right breast Lumpectomy surgeries in the same right breast and lymph nodes removed from my right armpit. Because the surgeon was not able to remove enough samples from the first surgery. She opened me up on the same incision less than two weeks after.

I am not sure why she was not able to take enough samples from the first lumpectomy surgery, but the second lumpectomy surgery in the same right breast was scheduled. This time I already knew what to do and what to expect. I signed the standard hospital waiver that the hospital, doctors, nurses, etc are not liable should something unexpected happens to me in the operating room.

On the operating table, I really was not completely healed yet from the first lumpectomy surgery but the second surgery needed to be done right away. Before I even finished counting 1 to 10, I was completely out at number 3 from the anesthesia.

The surgeon left color coded clips in my right breast and right armpit lymph nodes where they removed samples to identify where the cancer was. I woke up in the recovery room where my daughter Megan was waiting. This surgery, like the first one, was an out of patient surgery. So, after I was completely awake and able to move, I was released from the hospital. Again, I was told what to do and what not to do. Avoid lifting things for a few days, do not shower until after 24 hours, etc.

Then we happily went home. Just like last surgery, I did not want to go to bed without taking a shower and washing my hair first. I am not supposed to shower until after 24 hours but I showered anyway.

So, I wrapped both of my breasts with Saran Wrap again so the water would not be able to penetrate through the bandages and caused an infection. I am always thinking of what would happen if infection sets in.

Although everyone was nice and friendly at the hospital, It was a place that I do not want to be at anymore. I don't think anybody would!

The Healing and Recovery Time from my two Lumpectomy Surgeries:

I had plenty of rest. I took it really easy for the first few days. I did not do anything but watch TV, listen to music and eat.

I ate a well balanced meal: Meat, carbs, vegetables, fruits, nuts, plenty of water and liquid to drink.

Extra Strength Tylenol was my choice for pain. I only took the prescription pain reliever twice and I stopped taking them because it was giving me headaches and nausea.

I wore sports bras for full breast support even when I was sleeping. I felt like it restricted my movement.

I slept on the other side (left side) where I did not have the lumpectomy. It was very uncomfortable for the first few days.

The lumpectomy surgery itself was not painful because I was under anesthesia but the pain started the night after the surgery.

The recovery time for me was over a week. But I still prevented myself from lifting things after a week.

I started doing simple arm exercises but I could not raise my right arm all the way up because of the lymph nodes removed in my right armpit.

Remember I had 2 breast lumpectomies in my right breast because the breast cancer surgeon was not able to remove enough cell samples the first time. And, lymph nodes were removed in my right armpit during the second lumpectomy as well.

I asked my doctor why I can't move my right arm fully. She said it is from the lymph nodes removal in my right armpit. Then, she recommended physical therapy. So, I called and scheduled to meet with a physical therapist at the same hospital but in a different building.

So, the diagnosis was I have breast cancer in my right breast. It is stage 0. The cancer was caught at a very early stage. My doctor told me that having the mammogram twice actually gave them the best decision to get rid of this cancer.

The surgeon removed a lot of lymph nodes in my right armpit during this second breast lumpectomy as well. I am still Blessed and lucky that they found this cancer in a very early stage because of my routine mammogram.

The next procedure after the two lumpectomy surgeries will be right breast radiation to get rid of the cancer completely. Well after a few days after my lymph nodes in my right armpit were removed, I started having pain in my right armpit and right arm. And, I couldn't raise my arm all the way up. That's when my breast cancer surgeon recommended that I see a physical therapist.

So, I saw a very nice physical therapist at the same hospital but in a different building. She said that it is normal for a patient not to be able to raise the arm completely after lymph nodes removal from the armpit.

So, I started my physical therapy the same night that I saw her. They have little exercise equipment especially made for just hand and arm exercises. My physical therapy lasted for a few weeks but after 11 years, I still don't have a 100% range of motion in my right arm. And, I am just living with it now.

My First Right Breast Cancer Radiation Therapy

The next procedure after the two lumpectomy surgeries was right breast radiation for 2 months everyday, Monday through Friday. It started In December 2010 and ended in February 2011. I went in for my radiation early in the morning everyday before I went to work.

All the doctors, nurses, technicians, and receptionists at the Edward-Elmhurst Hospital's cancer center were very compassionate, kind, nice, and accommodating.

I can't tell you how grateful I am to all of them. They made my regular trip to the hospital's cancer center as pleasant as it could be for those two months.

I have always been scared of needles and I have never been a fan of tattoos. One of the radiation technicians asked my permission to put four dots of tattoos around my right breast so the radiation machine will be exact in pointing to cancer.

I agreed hesitantly just so the radiation machine will be focused on killing the cancer cells instead of killing the good and healthy cells. I still have those tattoos but they are not as bad as I thought they would be. They are small enough like regular moles.

"Radiation therapy is a treatment that uses high-energy radiation to kill cancer cells and to shrink tumors". This procedure is painless and is done to kill remaining cancer after surgery. It also lowers the risk of cancer coming back.

With all the procedures I went through and still going through currently, radiation therapy is the easiest and most painless. I'm sure I was probably glowing during those two months because of the high radiation, but who cares! At least I am still alive and that's all that matters.

I was given ointments to rub my right breast and surrounding area so it will prevent my breast and surrounding area from burn marks. Getting personal here but, my right nipple's color did not match my left nipple until years after the last day of my radiation. Yes, I mean years. I'm good with that though. At least cancer has not come back in my right breast. It's not a matter of if but when cancer comes back in my right breast, mastectomy is the next procedure that I have to go through. I am prepared for that.

Right Arm Physical Therapy

While I was going through the right breast radiation, I was also going through physical therapy for my right arm at the same hospital, but in a different building. I started my right arm physical therapy as soon as I noticed that I didn't have a 100% ROM (range of motion) in my right arm because of the number of lymph nodes removed in my right armpit. I could not move my right arm normally like before the surgery.

The physical therapy department had small equipment exclusively for hand and arm exercises that helped me bring back the feelings in my right arm and right armpit. In one of the early therapy sessions, I actually heard the physical therapist snap a lymph node that got tangled in my right armpit by pulling my right arm upward. She said sometimes this happens during the surgery and lymph nodes get tangled up.

It was really weird because we both heard the snapping sound.

It sounded like something that was broken into two pieces. Actually, I felt better right after that. My right arm and right armpit weren't as painful as after the surgery.

So, the tangled-up lymph nodes are the ones causing the pain in my right armpit and right arm. It was also the reason why I couldn't raise my right arm completely.

I continued my therapy for a few more weeks until I was able to move my right arm with less pain. But, as I said, unfortunately, I still don't have 100% ROM (range of motion). I am okay with that, though. At least I am still alive!

It has been eleven years now since that surgery and I still can't move and raise my right arm 100% completely and I just have to live with it now.

I now suffer from lymphedema on my right arm because of the lymph nodes removal. When I am at the hospital and the cancer center, the nurses take my blood pressure, pulse, etc. on my left arm now because it will not give them an accurate result if It was taken from my right arm.

I wear compression arm sleeves and compression gloves when I can't tolerate the pain, especially at night. I just take some Extra Strength Tylenol for pain. I learned to live with it now and truly appreciate that I am still kicking!

Playing golf has been at the top of my list of pleasure and enjoyment since the 1980s and I played a lot every time I had the chance. I even have a golf balls collection of golf courses that I played at and golf balls given to me by friends and people that I played with and against.

But, cancer and chemotherapy treatments' side effects put a stop or shall I say put a hold on that sport that I absolutely love for now! I am still hopeful that one of these days I will be able to be out on the golf course again, enjoying the open green course, playing with my best bud Beth and swinging my favorite golf clubs to my heart's content. GOD willing!

Side Effects of my First Right Breast Cancer

Most of the side effects from my first breast cancer were tolerable except for my lymphedema in my right arm (results of lymph nodes removed from my right armpit) which I still suffer from to this day.

It is now difficult for me to lift things using my right arm and hand. I am right-handed, so sometimes I tend to overuse my left arm and hand. I wear compression sleeves and compression gloves to ease the pain. Extra Strength Tylenol is now my go-to pain medication, instead of the prescription ones which are known to have many side effects including drug addiction.

Here are the side effects of my right breast cancer radiation:

1. Fatigue. I got tired easily.

2. I felt like my right breast was heavy at times.

3. It did not matter what lotion I applied around my right breast. It still felt dry and itchy at times.

4. My right breast nipple had a burnt color that did not match my left breast nipple for years after the radiation was over.

5. On the plus side, the radiation was not painful at all.

CHAPTER 3: MY FIRST COLORECTAL COLONOSCOPY

W hile I was waiting for the next procedure after the second lumpectomy surgery, I prepared myself for my first scheduled colorectal colonoscopy on 11/12/2010. This wasn't because of my breast cancer, but because of my age. I was getting older and was due for this procedure. Also, I think my doctors at this point were really concerned and wanted to keep a close eye on me health-wise.

I found out that the preparation for this procedure is worse than the actual colonoscopy. I drank what seemed like gallons of chalky stuff the night before the procedure. It is important to note that even though the chalky stuff comes in different flavors, it still tastes like chalk. Mine was cherry flavored, so it tasted like cherry chalk.

However, I discovered a trick on how to drink this nasty stuff without throwing up. Pinch your nose while drinking it and let out a big sigh of relief after taking a gulp. It helped me and I am sure it will help others too! After about 20 minutes or so I went to the bathroom several times to completely flush out my bowels. My stomach needed to be cleaned, free of food, etc so it would give accurate results on my colonoscopy.

I went in for a colonoscopy on 11/12/2010 at Edward-Elmhurst Hospital. Before the procedure started, there were two nurses and a doctor inside the colonoscopy room. The doctor asked me about my name, date of birth, and things that I am allergic to. I said I am allergic to cigarette smoke, cats, and mold. So, the doctor asked everyone including me if everyone was ready. We all said yes and the doctor paused and said by the way we have to make sure that, **"that there is no smoking cat in the room while Nora is having a colonoscopy"**. Everyone started laughing including me and then I was completely out. To this day, that is still one of the funniest things that I have ever heard. It really put me at ease too.

The actual procedure only took about maybe 15 to 20 minutes. I did not feel a thing. I was completely out. The colonoscopy doctor read the results and told me that there was no cancer and that I should have a colonoscopy done every six years. Finally, some good news!

This is an out-of-patient procedure and should be done for people over 50 years old every 6 years. I highly recommend colonoscopy to everyone, whether you are healthy or not, and maybe even before 50 years old, you should have this procedure. All you have to do is get through the chalky stuff!

My close friend from college, Frocie, died of colon cancer at the young age of 48 years old. She left behind an 8-year-old son and a husband. My first cousin, Ellen also died of colon cancer at a young age and left a husband and children. Colonoscopy was not really talked about during that time yet. It probably would have saved both their lives if they both had that procedure done. Colon cancer, according to doctors, is the easiest cancer to treat if diagnosed early. We always have to remember that early cancer detection is the only key to survival! I am living proof of that and so are my cancer survivor friends! So, please have your mammogram and colonoscopy done as soon as possible.

My Second Colorectal Colonoscopy 2016

You may recall that my first colorectal colonoscopy was in 2010. Well, I was due for my second one because of how closely I am being monitored due to my cancer history and also because it has been six years already. They did not find any cancer in my colon the first time and they just wanted to make sure that there was no cancer in my colon this time too. As we all know, the preparation for this procedure is more significant than the actual colonoscopy. Remember the drinking of the nasty chalky stuff? Which seemed like gallons and gallons of it (I am exaggerating)? I was back to chugging it all over again.

Just like what I did the first time and the second time, I drank this stuff also when I had my ovarian cancer and hysterectomy surgery the day after Thanksgiving 2011. Well, my trick was to pinch my nose and drink this nasty chalky stuff until it is gone and let out a sigh of relief after. It worked then and it certainly worked again this time.

Prior to the colonoscopy procedure, I encountered another problem. Not one of the nurses present was certified and qualified to access my power port for the anesthesia to run through. One of the nurses tried to poke me in the very fine vein in my arm and she failed. My vein burst! That is the whole reason why I have a power port. So, the doctor asked a nurse from another department to help out. By this time the doctor was losing his patience since he was on such a tight schedule.

This was the same doctor who performed my first colonoscopy and the same doctor who made a joke about my allergies to cigarette smoke and cats. He had a good sense of humor then, but at that moment, not so much. If I was not so tense at that moment, I would have made a joke myself.

That was exactly the reason why I wanted my colonoscopy done at Edward-Elmhurst main hospital in Naperville. But this doctor insisted that the Plainfield location was equipped just as well. He just did not think about my powerport which he was totally aware of.

Now, the actual colorectal colonoscopy procedure is only supposed to take about 15 to 20 minutes long. But, I had to wait for a nurse who was certified and qualified to access my power port, which took over one hour. What a waste of everybody's time!

The results of my second colonoscopy were good. Like my first colonoscopy results, there was no cancer. So the doctor suggested I go for my third colonoscopy after six years. I am already scheduled to have my third colonoscopy in September 2022 at the same hospital, Edward-Elmhurst Hospital. I am not looking forward to chugging the chalky stuff again though but it needs to get done so it will be done!

CHAPTER 4: THE SECOND FLOOR OF THE CANCER CENTER

My radiation procedures were done at the cancer center's radiation department, which is located on the first floor of the building. One day, I asked Kimmie, the nice, kind, and compassionate first-floor receptionist (who later became one of my friends), what is on the second floor of this building? She said in a serious voice that that was a place where you do not want to be at. Which only made me even more curious! From the outside of the glass building, I could see a baby grand piano and I heard a pianist playing beautiful music. I again asked what is on the second floor. She responded in a serious voice that it is the chemotherapy department.

My jaw just dropped and I felt nauseated because my own mother was misdiagnosed with throat cancer that supposedly showed on the right side of her neck in the early 1970s. She underwent cobalt radiation and chemotherapy treatments and suffered from all the side effects of chemotherapy which caused her right side shoulder, right arm and right hand to be frozen for well over thirty years. I have seen the devastating side effects of chemotherapy through my mother. It was very painful to witness. My siblings and I were not prepared to watch our mom suffer from all the side effects of chemotherapy that she had but did not need.

It all started when my parents had a picnic with my father's siblings and in-laws. One of my aunts, who was a family doctor, noticed that my mom's right side of the neck was different from the left side. My mom was not in pain and did not feel anything different. But, since her sister-law was a family doctor, she thought she better listen to her.

So, she advised my mom to have it checked out. My mom did exactly what my aunt suggested and that was the start of her terrible experience. Her life was turned upside down.

My mom was diagnosed by one greedy and power hungry doctor in the Philippines with throat cancer that was apparently visible in the right side of her neck. But we did not see what the doctor was talking about. My mom's neck was normal in size and color. She was not having problems swallowing either.

Like what I said earlier, because my mom and her children were intimidated by that doctor, we were not given the opportunity to seek another doctor's opinion. I don't remember seeing the supposedly lump in her right side of the neck nor did my dad and siblings. My mom was not in pain and did not feel anything different. But we trusted that SOB doctor because he should know better. So, my mom underwent cobalt radiation and chemotherapy treatments shortly after that. And, suffered from all the side effects including hair loss, vomiting, constipation, nauseated, etc. which we all thought was from cancer and not chemotherapy treatments. That's how naive and ignorant we all were about cancer. Her supposedly cancer was the first in my family. Her doctor/oncologist took advantage of my mom's trust in him and my parents money and it definitely showed how uninformed we all were about cancer.

I said she was misdiagnosed because she was examined in Los

Angeles, California in the 1980s and according to her oncologist in California, she never had cancer!

There was no trace of cancer in her body. Every time I think of what she went through all those years and all the side effects of chemotherapy that she did not need, it makes me very angry that her oncologist took advantage of her and us. My dad, my siblings, and I suffered with our mom. They took the good quality of life my mom had before that wrong diagnosis.

My mother Mely was an incredibly kind, generous, and strong woman who took care of her 6 children on her own when my father Federico, Sr. died unexpectedly of a heart attack and stroke at a very young age of 50 years old. When my dad died people thought it was my mom that died because she was the one with supposed cancer.

Then they were all shocked and surprised when they read my dad's obituary in the newspaper. I believe that my mom's misdiagnosis of cancer contributed to my dad's early death. My parents were not wealthy. They were an average family but they both always helped and thought of others first.

Seeing my mom reduced to being dependent on others most of the time for well over thirty years was devastating, to say the least. After being in and out of the hospital for many years not because of cancer but because she was getting old, my kind and beautiful mom died of pneumonia in a nursing home in Chicago, IL in June of 2004. She was 77 years old. May she rest in peace!

My oldest sister Tess was diagnosed with breast cancer and went through mastectomy surgery, radiation, and chemotherapy the awful side effects included: losing one of her breasts, hair loss, etc. in the 1980s. She did not ask another doctor for a second opinion. No other blood tests or other tests were done. Instead, she relied on, trusted, and believed in one greedy and dishonest doctor that was referred to her by one of her friends. Right off the bat, her doctor recommended removing one of her breasts which she agreed to with no hesitation because she wanted to be around her very young sons and her husband for many years.

Who knows if she really did need to go through all of that? I believed that she would have lived for many years even without that promise from that greedy and selfish doctor anyway. And she lived a full and productive life and was able to help a lot of people for over 30 years after that. Until she died of a heart attack and stroke unexpectedly in June 2018. She was 67 years old.

I remember having a conversation with my sister Tess about this topic years ago. I did not blame her for not doing more research before she underwent a mastectomy and the treatments she had as she already suffered enough. But I thought to myself, didn't she remember what our mother went through? To this day, I really still don't believe that my sister Tess ever had breast cancer. Again, like my mom, she went through all the physical, mental, emotional, and financial pain and everything for nothing!

They both suffered so much in the hands of those greedy, power-hungry, and dishonest Filipino doctors. I am referring to those two greedy and power-hungry doctors only. I am not talking about all Filipino doctors because I have a whole slew of relatives that are medical doctors and they are all well respected by their peers, patients, and others.

I love and miss my mom and my sister Tess so much and it upsets me to think about what they both endured, especially if they didn't need to go through it in the first place.

Needless to say, the second floor of the cancer center scared me. Kimmie was right, that was not a place that I ever wanted to go. Cancer terrified me. Chemotherapy terrified me. Little did I know that I would end up going to the second floor more times than I could even try to count.

CHAPTER 5: SECOND CANCER, AGGRESSIVE METASTATIC OVARIAN

Exactly five months after my last breast cancer radiation in February 2011. I woke up one morning in July 2011 feeling very bloated. It felt like the food that I ate for dinner last night was just sitting in the upper part of my stomach and hadn't been digested. I started feeling the pain too. I did not think anything of it, but it persisted for days, weeks, and months ahead. So, I made an appointment to see my previous primary doctor. At the time when I saw him, I was feeling pain in my lower stomach constantly.

My stomach looked bigger and heavier than when I was pregnant with my own daughter Megan. I was really big when I was pregnant and I could not see my feet when I was standing. My ex-husband Jim literally had to tie my shoes before he went to work. That was how big my stomach was then, but I was even bigger in 2011. I was gaining a lot of weight but just in my stomach area, while the rest of my body was normal. With all the signs that I had, I thought my primary doctor would do a little more checking and testing but he did not.

The doctor came into the room and I told him what I was feeling.

He looked at me and said that I am just gaining weight because I am getting older. He also said I was probably bloating because I would often eat oatmeal for breakfast. So, he told me to go home, lose some weight and not worry about it. I went home but I was still in pain. The pain was especially bad at night when I lay in bed. The hot water bottle that I placed on top of my stomach every night to ease the pain wasn't working anymore. It was a pain that I couldn't get rid of. I know my body and I know something was wrong with me.

Here I thought he is a doctor so he knows what he is talking about, right? No, I think it was him who was getting older and getting senile. Although he was aware of my medical history, especially my right breast cancer, two lumpectomies, and radiation that I just went through months ago, he should have ordered for me to have some blood tests but he did not.

He was a lazy and incompetent doctor at that time. While thinking about it one night, like a lightning bolt, I vividly remembered that this was the same doctor who had his nurse inject me with steroids to get rid of my poison ivy poisoning months prior. Then, ordered me to have my blood drawn for cholesterol a day after the steroids. I asked his nurse if it would alter the results of my blood test. She asked the doctor and the doctor said no, it will not. Guess what? He was absolutely wrong! The results of the blood tests showed that I was diabetic which I wasn't. So, just as I suspected, the steroid shot altered the results.

He then still ordered me to attend a class for people with diabetes at the hospital. So, like a good patient, I did go to the diabetic class. The first thing the speaker of that diabetic class said was that if we were exposed to steroids then it would give false positive results. They took my blood sugar before the class and my blood sugar was normal. She said that I do not have diabetes. I went and saw my primary doctor a few days after the class at the clinic and showed him the blood test results.

The patient is not diabetic it said. That patient was me. I told him the steroid you had your nurse inject me with was the cause of the false positive results. He did not respond to me, instead, he said I can go home now without apologizing to me for his incompetence. I just could not believe that this is the same primary doctor I trusted for 10 years.

At that moment, I was so frustrated, disappointed, angry, and annoyed with this doctor. I left his office, went home, and started calling doctors in my insurance network to replace this incompetent primary doctor that I had for 10 years. At this point, I was still in constant pain. You may recall that his advice to me was to go home, nothing's wrong with you. Lose some weight! You are just getting older and gaining weight? He was still hell-bent on believing that I was just getting older and gaining weight.

The Diagnosis

After calling so many doctors, I found a doctor that was included in my health insurance doctors network that would accept my insurance. Her name was Dr. Carol Weinberg, MD, primary doctor. By now, it was 4 months after I first started feeling the pain. She asked what the problem was and asked me to see her that same day in the afternoon. That was the Monday in November 2011 before Thursday, Thanksgiving Day.

I got to her office around 5:30 pm. She examined me and told me to go to the hospital immediately for a priority series of procedures and blood tests that she ordered. I saw her worried face. I just knew something was wrong with me but she couldn't tell me yet without the blood test results.

She promised to call me at home to tell me the results and she said it doesn't matter if it was midnight or early in the morning. So, I went directly to Edward-Elmhurst Hospital. The hospital knew I was coming because Dr. Weinberg's office called them.

A nurse escorted me to change into a hospital gown and the blood tests started followed by a PET scan, etc. It was already late at night when all the procedures were done and the nurse let me go home and wait for the test results at home.

My phone rang around 11:30 pm. I grabbed the phone and started listening to her. She said is your daughter with you? I said yes, she's here. She said I want you both seated, put me on speaker phone, and listen. She said I just got your test results and you have another cancer and I want both of you in my office tomorrow, Tuesday, so we can discuss what to do next. After hearing the word cancer, I didn't understand any of the words she said after that. My brain just went totally blank. Megan picked up the phone and finished the conversation with the doctor.

After Megan hung up the phone, we both just started crying... sobbing, and held each other tight like it was the end of the world. And, to me in all honesty, it felt like It was the end of my world! I could not comprehend why I have another cancer when my first cancer right breast cancer was only stage 0. And, I was able to get rid of it. I was in remission from that cancer. I guess in a way, I was in denial that I would have another cancer. I was not aware that my cancer would jump from one part of my body to another. But, it did!

I think that moment was the most emotional I had been in my whole entire life. The physical, mental and emotional pain I was suffering and experiencing over the last few months was real.

I just needed someone to tell me that I was correct. I wasn't making it up like what my previous primary doctor was telling me.

All I remember was Megan telling me, "you will be ok, Mom! We will fight and win this battle with cancer again like we did the first one!" I knew that we were both very upset and emotional that night but we have to believe in something. I survived the first breast cancer and I had to believe that I would survive this one, too!

On the Tuesday before Thanksgiving in November 2011, Megan and I were at my new primary doctor's clinic. Remember, I just met this doctor the night before. She was a very thorough and caring doctor. She repeated what she told us over the phone the night before that I have another cancer, this time it was ovarian cancer. This explained why I was having constant pain in my stomach area for months. I went numb and became speechless. I couldn't hear or understand anything, let alone ask any questions.

Luckily, Megan was able to keep it together enough to remember what was said to us. She took a hold of my hand & told me that we were going to get through this. Then she asked the doctor how big the tumor was and the doctor told me, "imagine putting toothpaste on a toothbrush and smearing it on the inside of a glass. That's how much cancer is inside of you right now". She further explained that I would need surgery right away.

She recommended Dr. Potkul, the Head of Ovarian Cancer Surgery at Loyola Medical Center in Maywood. I told her that I preferred a surgeon in our town so that it would be closer. She said that this surgeon was her friend, so she was able to ask him for a big favor to help me out because I needed emergency surgery. She also said that he was the best of the best. So, I agreed to see the surgeon in another town because of my new primary doctor's recommendation. After all, she was the one who discovered my ovarian cancer. I owe her a ton of gratitude!

She also recommended Dr. Hantel, Head of Oncology Department at the Cancer Center of Edward-Elmhurst Hospital in Naperville for chemotherapy treatments after the surgery.

I can't remember the rest of the conversation but I vividly remember her wishing me the best of luck.

Consultation with Dr. Potkul, MD

I had my first appointment with Dr. Potkul on Wednesday, the day before Thanksgiving November 2011. Before the appointment, I picked up my ultrasound, x-ray, etc from Edward-Elmhurst Hospital in Naperville, IL for the surgeon to view and read. During that year we didn't have the luxury of emailing the test results yet. Then, Megan and I met the surgeon in Maywood, IL in the afternoon. He was a very nice doctor.

I had blood tests again and other procedures at this hospital, Loyola Medical Center, before the doctor discussed things with me and Megan. Then after a couple of hours, the results came out.

He said it looked like a huge cancer in my stomach area, left side, and part of my back that consisted of many tumors. When we asked him how big the biggest tumor was he made a fist and said that it was bigger than a softball. The doctor said that he would do everything he could to remove all the cancer. He was a very professional, mild-mannered, and straight-to-the-point kind of person. He actually gave me a good sense of courage to be well prepared for what I was about to go through. Meanwhile, he said that he wanted me to enjoy a great Thanksgiving dinner with my family and that I'd have the surgery first thing Friday morning.

When we got home, I called the hospital to schedule my emergency surgery. The wonderful lady who answered the phone said **"Ma'am, I don't know if you believe in GOD but, I will pray to my GOD for your successful surgery and quick recovery"**. Hearing that from a total stranger made me happy and emotional as well. She was so kind and sincere. I hope that she is doing well in life. To this day, it still gives me goosebumps every time I think of that moment. There are still so many incredibly kind souls out there. I always try my very best to return the favor by showing kindness and helping others as well every chance I get.

What I thought was my Last Thanksgiving Dinner

On Thanksgiving 2011, Jim, my ex-husband, and Megan prepared a simple but nice Thanksgiving dinner. You know the usual roasted turkey, mashed potatoes, sweet potatoes, vegetables, dinner rolls, and dessert. Here, I was thinking that this might be my last Thanksgiving dinner but I did not tell Megan or Jim. Maybe they were also thinking of the same thing. I thought that was the most delicious dinner I ever had!

I ate enough only to drink that chalky stuff after a couple of hours, to get rid of all the food I just ate and enjoyed. My stomach needed to be completely empty before the morning of major surgery. I knew the drill on how to drink this chalky stuff by now. Pinched my nose, drank this chalky stuff and breathed a sigh of relief.

As I was running back and forth to the bathroom, I received numerous phone calls from friends and family who wished me the best of luck on my ovarian cancer surgery. They were all so worried about me. I was so appreciative and thankful for all of them but, here I was thinking please just let me go to the bathroom! Haha! Thinking about it now, they were more worried about me than I was worried about myself. It may seem funny then but, they were right.

Meanwhile, I updated my living will for Megan to have just in case something happens to me on the operating table. I do that every time I go for surgery now.

And, there were many times. I revised my living will every single time. It's better to always be prepared.

Stage 4 Aggressive Metastatic Ovarian Cancer Surgery

My ovarian cancer surgery was the day after Thanksgiving. Jim picked me and Megan up very early Friday morning to avoid traffic. At the hospital, I signed the usual standard waiver that the hospital, doctors, nurses, etc are not liable if something happens unexpectedly to me at the operating table.

Then, I was admitted and taken to my room. They got me ready and wheeled me in the operating room. After the anesthesia, I really do not remember anything else. I had a feeling that I was at the operating table for many hours. I just did not know how long until Megan said the nurses told them that I was in the operating room for at least over 7 hours. It was really bright and sunny when they took me to the operating room that morning and It was already very dark when they transferred me to my room that night.

After the surgery, they put me in the recovery room. I was told the cancer was so big and the surgeon and his medical team were not able to remove all the cancer. I prayed and hoped that they would be able to remove all the cancer. I also had a hysterectomy during that ovarian cancer surgery. I thought it was okay and at least I made it out of the operating room alive. Since the surgeon and his team were not able to remove all the cancer because of its size, chemotherapy was next for me.

The hospital staff that morning told Megan and Jim to go home and they would call them when I was already out of the operating room and back in my room. Boy, was I happy to see both of them. At least I know I was still alive!

After they left the hospital that night, one of the nurses told me that I have control of the morphine drip in my vein for pain. So, if I am in pain all I have to do is adjust the drip. I can vividly remember asking the nurse jokingly if I could overdose on this morphine drip. She said no because it's controlled. I said, "thank goodness because I just survived the very long hours of surgery and I don't feel like dying just yet!" She started laughing. I was glad to see that I could still make people laugh even in my hospital bed!

I was in the hospital for three days from Friday morning to Sunday night when they let me go home. Megan and Jim were at the hospital with me every day. They were in my hospital room when the nurse told me that I could go home that Sunday night. That made me very happy.

I was also told that my ovarian cancer (CA125) level before the surgery was 4000 U/mL. And, after the surgery it went down to 2000 U/mL. Normal is less than 35 U/mL. This is how they measure the cancer levels in your body when it comes to ovarian cancer. If your levels are above normal then that means that you have ovarian cancer, whereas, if the level is below average, you're basically in the clear. Try to remember the number 4000 U/mL because I will discuss this in detail later.

Since the cancer was so big it affected not only my stomach area and ovaries but also my left side and part of my back as well. Despite the long hours of surgery and the huge size of the cancer, my surgeon, unfortunately, wasn't able to remove all the cancer. It was just impossible to remove everything. Due to the length of surgery over seven hours, I lost a lot of blood. So, I had blood transfusions during the surgery. I would also end up having more blood transfusions during some of my chemotherapy treatments as well. The surgeon left numerous colored clips in my pelvis area where the cancer was. I am so thankful and grateful for Dr. Putkol and his medical team.

Meanwhile, my best friend Beth, her family and parents were all so worried about me. So was my good friend Luz, my sisters Tess and Lynne, brother Rico and their families as well. The emotional, moral and spiritual support from all of them was incredibly touching and unbelievable! To say I love them all so much is an understatement!!!

The next plan was chemotherapy treatment to get rid of the leftover cancer which I will discuss in detail later. At this point because of what I had seen first hand with my mom's experience suffering from the side effects of chemo, I was petrified!

My mom's side effects were: Hair loss (her hair was literally falling out and on her white pillow case at her hospital bed), no appetite, constantly vomiting, weight loss, etc. She even contemplated suicide to end her pain and suffering by jumping off the hospital building.

Her room was on the fifth floor of the hospital if I remember it correctly. Luckily, some of my siblings and I were there to stop her. We were able to convince her to think and focus on her recovery for us, her children. We all saw her suffering physically but we were not really aware of her mental and emotional feelings during that time.

My mom's cancer experience was the first in my immediate family. That was in the early 1970's. So, we really did not know what to expect. The hair loss we thought was from her cancer and not from the chemotherapy side effects. We were all so uninformed about cancer. Her doctor/oncologist never really explained to us what we all, especially my mom, needed to know. Thinking about it now, I think her doctor/oncologist did it intentionally for us not to be given the correct information and for all of us to just rely on whatever he said.

Knowing what we eventually came to know, we were all just so naive and maybe even afraid to ask questions to not offend her doctor/oncologist. When in reality that SOB doctor/oncologist was a liar, greedy, selfish and just after my mom's money.

Now, back to me, after the initial shock and being petrified, I said to myself this is just another challenge in my cancer journey. My mom was in the early 1970's. I am sure that the technology nowadays is way more advanced than it was forty years ago.

So, chemotherapy, bring it on, I was ready with no hesitation! I just wanted to get it over within the shortest possible days.

Not knowing that chemotherapy and its side effects are different for different patients. It's not a one size fits all kind of thing. By this time, I was in and out of the hospital so many times that I stopped counting. There was a time when I referred to Edward-Elmhurst Hospital and Cancer Center as my second home!

Consultation with Dr. Alex Hantel, MD, System Medical Director, Oncology Services

It was now December 2011. Just days after my major ovarian cancer and hysterectomy surgery from Loyola Medical Center. My surgical incision was longer than a ruler. And, with the metal staples still attached to my skin, Megan and I met with Dr. Hantel, my ovarian cancer oncologist and the most caring, greatest and kindest oncologist on this planet!

To him, his cancer patients are not just numbers, it is personal to him! My new primary doctor, Dr. Carol Weinberg, MD recommended him to me just like how she recommended my ovarian cancer surgeon, Dr. Potkul.

The hospital where he works is just about 3 miles away from my house. Dr. Hantel is the head of the Oncology Department at the cancer center of Edward-Elmhurst Hospital in Naperville, IL. He discussed with us his plans of treatments for me. Right off the bat he said that there is no cure for cancer but it is treatable! He wanted me to get started with chemotherapy as soon as possible.

I asked him if I should wait until I fully recovered from the surgery. But, he said no because of the size of my cancer. Leftover cancer needed to be eradicated immediately and it could not wait. The sooner we took care of the leftover cancer the better it would be for me. At that point, I trusted Dr. Hantel, MD 100%. Because he seemed like an honest person and he looked so trustworthy! He also has an excellent reputation among cancer patients, doctors, nurses, and staff.

Welcome to my new world of more medical procedures and doctor's visits! Actually, as I said before, there was a time when I considered Edward-Elmhurst Hospital as my second home for years because I was always there for medical procedures on a weekly and monthly basis. I came to know my doctors, nurses, laboratory technicians, receptionists, social workers, and medical staff. I really think being compassionate is part of the requirements to work in that hospital because they are all so compassionate and kind. I appreciated that so much.

Remember, I started going there with my very first cancer. Right breast cancer in 2010. Procedures are done like needle biopsies, chemotherapy, colonoscopy, surgeries, radiation, mammograms, PET scans, MRIs, bone scans, ultrasounds, thyroid scans, EKGs, physical therapy, etc. It is now 2021 and I am still going to the cancer center and Edward-Elmhurst Hospital for some of those procedures. I can probably close my eyes and drive to the hospital without getting lost.

Removal of my Surgical Incision's Metal Staples

It was still December 2011, Megan and I went back to Loyola Medical Center where I had my ovarian cancer and hysterectomy surgery, for another doctor to remove the metal staples from my surgical incision.

Remember my surgical incision was longer than a ruler. To give you a better idea, the surgical incision was from my breastbone down to the top of my vagina. It was a big cancer so the incision was big too. The metal staples had to be removed before they attached permanently to my skin. I was a little nervous, but at the same time, I was curious to see my healing progress.

That was the first time I saw my body without the bandage wrapped around my body. I felt like throwing up and nauseated seeing how big and long the surgical incision was.

But, not once did I ask myself why me. Instead, I asked myself why not me. I was positive and confident enough to tackle everything thrown at me at this point. This is just another of the many challenges that I had to overcome. And, I kept telling myself that I would get through this!

You can just imagine how many metal staples there were. When the first metal staple was removed and dropped in a metal bowl, it made this loud noise that will stay in my memory forever. The rest of the metal staples were removed and one by one dropped in that metal bowl.

The female doctor made it looked like it was nothing. It seemed like she had done this process one too many times already. Megan was in the same room with me. I knew that she was feeling uncomfortable like me but she did not say anything. She was very patient just waiting for the whole thing to get over with.

"Couldn't they just use soluble plastic staples?", I asked myself. No, because the surgical incision was too big and too long. The incision will just open up if it was plastic. I remember asking that doctor how long my incision was. She told me, upon seeing my scared and pale face, that they didn't measure the size of the incision. Of course, they do. She just didn't want to tell me. But I measured the length of the incision at home myself. The length was longer than a ruler. So it was over twelve inches long.

During the process of removing the metal staples, I just closed my eyes and just thought of good things to keep my mind off the uncomfortable feeling I was having at that time. It hurt a little because the surgical scars haven't fully dried yet. Some of the metal staples still had my flesh on them. Then the room went totally silent. The last staple was removed. It was only then that I opened my eyes, looked at the incision, and a quick sigh of relief. I then looked at the metal staples in the metal bowl.

Then the doctor wrapped my entire upper body with a fresh bandage again to prevent the surgical incision from opening up. And, we were sent home. Before leaving the hospital, the doctor told me to rest and take it easy for a few weeks.

And, I wasn't allowed to drive for a couple of months until I was fully healed to prevent my surgical incision from opening up and getting infected. But, 13 days after my ovarian cancer and hysterectomy surgery, I started getting bored from not doing anything. I got so bored that I went back to work. I could work because as an accountant my work is all using a computer and not doing any lifting work, but I just couldn't drive yet. I am the type of person who is always doing something and always on the go so, staying home for weeks just watching TV, eating, not being able to exercise, and doing nothing else was a waste of time as far as I was concerned.

CHAPTER 6: MY FIRST CHEMOTHERAPY

I t was still December 2011 when I started my first chemotherapy treatments. I was given instructions on what it would be like to go through chemotherapy, blood transfusions, the side effects, the food I needed to eat (protein, fruits and vegetables are on top of the list), drink plenty of water, plenty of rest, do some exercise if I could. Also, what to do and who to call if I felt sick even in the middle of the night. My chemotherapy treatments were every Friday one hour each session for four and a half months. This went from December 2011 to April 13, 2012. So, the number 13 has been my favorite number since then because my chemotherapy treatments ended on the 13th of April 2012. And, yes it was a Friday. So, Friday the 13th!

My first chemotherapy treatment was at the cancer center of Edward-Elmhurst Hospital. By the way, before the chemotherapy, I signed a waiver that says that there is no guarantee that the chemotherapy will work for me. And it might even cause my death. At that point, I really didn't have any other choice. So, Megan and I checked in with the receptionist. Then a nurse came and took Megan and me to this huge room where there was a piano.

Remember, this was what I saw when I had radiation on my right breast on the first floor of this building. This is also the department where Kimmie, the receptionist, said I would not want to be. Well, there I was on the second floor. The nurse asked me if I wanted a private room or a chair in the big common room that overlooked a man-made pond. I thought since I have a choice I might as well choose a private room. The room had a big recliner chair that can be pushed all the way back like a bed for comfort, a TV, guest chairs, and the chemotherapy dispenser. We were also offered snacks and fruit juice/bottled water.

Then two nurses came in. They verified my name and some other personal information. One of them inserted the needle in my left arm and explained to me the kind of chemotherapy solutions carboplatin and paclitaxel that will go through my vein. I have very fine veins, which have ruptured before from nurses from another facility who tried to draw blood. I know that they did not mean it. But, those were very painful and traumatic experiences for me. The nurse assigned to me did a great job. She was gentle and it was like a quick sting in my vein. Thank God for her.

And, the nurse said that it will take about one hour for the process to finish. Before the chemotherapy solutions were released, the two nurses talked to each other and made sure that those were the correct chemotherapy solutions and dosage for me. One nurse verified and the other confirmed. I liked that they were very thorough and professional to avoid potentially deadly mistakes.

Then the chemotherapy started. They gave me a nice warm blanket and two pillows. I was able to close my eyes and prayed while Megan watched TV. I thought to myself, "wow, this chemo is easy." Because I did not have any side effects yet.

Well, I spoke too soon! That same night, I started vomiting. And, I did not feel like eating but I tried to eat something because

I needed to. Two days after that first round of chemo, some of my hair started falling out! I became constipated, vomited a few times, nauseated, felt light-headed, had headaches, and could not sleep.

Now, I realize that these are all side effects of chemotherapy. And, I would not want to wish this on my worst enemy. I pray and hope that someone will be able to invent a cancer treatment, if not a cure, that does not have all these awful side effects.

The great news was my ovarian cancer level went down from 4000U/mL before the surgery to 2000 U/mL after the surgery.

It went down from 2000 U/mL to around 20 U/mL after just the first few chemotherapy treatments. Again normal cancer level is below 35 U/mL. My ovarian cancer level was now within the normal level. That means my ovarian cancer was responding very well to the chemotherapy treatments. Megan and I were very happy and so was Dr. Hantel, MD. That was a tremendous Blessing! Thank GOD again!

Despite all the side effects, my ovarian cancer was responding very well to even just the first few rounds of chemotherapy. I prayed and hoped that it would continue to lower my ovarian cancer level and eradicate my cancer completely. So far so good!

Everytime I had chemotherapy treatments my ovarian cancer level would go down. Dr. Hantel and I noticed that every time I have another cancer my ovarian cancer level goes up. It has only gone up to less than 20 U/mL since then. And, it's still less than the standard less than 35 U/ml level. The results fluctuate which is still okay, I guess.

My Boredness Led Me Back To Work

Megan still couldn't drive because she had a severely sprained right ankle, so I was helped by a lot of caring and loving people, who I call my true friends and family.

They drove me and picked me up from my accounting clients' offices. They are my best bud Beth, my good friend Luz, my niece Marnie and my ex-husband, Jim. Luz was always there for us whether grocery shopping, driving us to wherever we wanted to go, etc.

It did not matter what time we called her she was always there for Megan and me.

Same with my best bud Beth and her family. They are there for Megan and me before, during, and after cancer. Marnie had given me a ride a few times and brought us food. Jim was there every time Megan called him.

Megan and I are blessed with such loving, caring, kind, and compassionate human beings. We owe all of them a ton of gratitude and I know we will not be able to repay them for what they did for us. But if they ever need our help, you bet we are going to be there for them as well!

It was also during this time when a whole lot of people were praying, offering masses, novenas intended for me and Megan. There are too many of you to mention but you all know who you are. Thank you very much to everyone!

After a couple of months, I was now able to drive myself to work. I did just fine but, I realized what our eyelashes are for. Remember one of the side effects of chemo is hair loss. I lost every single hair on my body including my eyelashes and eyebrows.

This was now the summer months. While I was driving I rolled down the windows and opened the sunroof. I needed that fresh air and wind. I took off my hat so my bald head was now exposed. I felt like every time I got to a stop light the other drivers were staring at me but I did not care. At least I was still alive.

I did not have my sunglasses on so the wind was directly hitting my face and the purpose of the eyelashes was to control the dust from entering our eyes. And, I put my sunglasses back on. I was good. The little things in life that we take for granted, now I realize that every single little thing has a purpose. I appreciate everything now.

Megan bought me a ton of hats to wear. But even with the hats, I stopped wearing them as soon as I had some hair growing out. I remember when Megan and I were at the cancer center once waiting for my name to be called for chemotherapy.

I sat behind an old lady with very thin white hair. We could actually see her scalp even with her hair. I think she was one of the cancer patients waiting to be called for her appointment or a caregiver. I was thinking I wish I had hair like hers even if it's thin. At least I'll have hair. I am going to say this one more time. At that moment, I learned to appreciate everything that we are given by GOD! Do not take anything for granted. Even simple and little things mean something to someone like me at that instance.

Parking Lot Incident...If Looks Can Kill

I really feel it's important that I should include this incident that happened to me. There's a valuable lesson learned here.

When I just first started driving again after my ovarian cancer surgery. I stopped by a Target store to get some paper products on my way back home from my accounting client's office. I parked my car on the second spot while the first and third spots were open. It was in the middle of the afternoon. So, it wasn't really busy.

After my quick shopping, I went back to my car and put the

shopping bags on the front passenger side because opening the trunk was difficult for me to open at that time. The first and third spots were still available at that moment. I was still moving so slowly because I was trying to protect my incision from opening up. Then a woman was driving so fast in the parking lot and quickly was going to park on the first spot while I was still standing on that spot.

I hurriedly moved in front of my car to avoid being run over by her. She got out of her car and stared at me without saying anything. She was probably asking herself why I was moving too slowly. I had a few choice words I wanted to say to her but I decided not to. I looked at her and I thought shall I even waste my energy in explaining to her why I was slowly moving?

I had very limited energy during that time because of the chemotherapy side effects. My patience was not up to par yet too. So, explaining it to her was out of the question. I tell you though, if looks can kill, I would have been dead instantly at that moment!

At that time there were a whole slew of parking spots available including the first spot on the other side but she wanted that first spot where I was standing, I guess!

So, I just gave her the benefit of the doubt. I did not say anything, got back in my car, and slowly drove away. Being kind to someone doesn't cost anything. Especially when we don't know what someone is going through. A little kindness goes a long way. Let's all keep that in mind!

Powerport Device Implant

Another surgery! Dr. Hantel told me that it would be best if I got a powerport device implant since they would need to access my veins so much because of the chemo. My body was now full of surgical scars. Now, the powerport device would also leave scars.

I remember when I went in for a follow-up mammogram (one of many every six months) since 2010, the new mammography technician made a comment that my body looked like a map because it is full of surgical scars. I said that I agreed, but at least I was still alive! She said yes, "that you are!"

The powerport surgery is a minor surgery where the patient is awake but injected with local anesthesia. That was the definition that I got from my search. But I vividly remember that the surgeon made me count from 1 to 10 and I was completely out at number 3. My surgery took about one hour and I was snoozing.

I did not feel anything during the surgery but I felt pain after a few hours of anesthesia wearing out. Also, I felt a little sore and heaviness on that side of my body for a few hours. I just had a couple of Extra Strength Tylenol after. It is an outpatient surgery. The powerport implanted device is a plastic or metal disc-shaped port about the size of a quarter that is implanted under my skin above my left breast and below my left shoulder bone. I am not sure if I have a metal or a plastic power port. I think I have a metal one.

The goal of the power port device is to have my blood drawn, blood transfusions, IV hookup, and most important for chemotherapy treatments instead of poking my very fine vein. Since, I am still being monitored and checked for my ovarian cancer level and blood tests on a regular basis, my powerport has helped me tremendously over the last ten years and counting not to have that awful traumatic experience again.

So, every time I go in for my regular ovarian cancer level and blood tests, I keep praying that the nurse assigned to me that particular day will be able to access my powerport easily with no problems. Most of the time, they are able to.

The Edward-Elmhurst Hospital cancer center nurses are all well trained and certified to access powerport devices and always make sure that every time they access my powerport, they flush it with saline and heparin (a blood thinner) to prevent the powerport from clogging. Within the last ten years that I have had this powerport, I think they only unclog it about six times. So, that is really good. This powerport device will stay in my body until I die and will take it to my grave.

Also, I can not go through metal detectors in airports and government buildings. They have to let me in on the side without the metal detectors. I have a special ID to show them that I have a powerport device implanted below my left shoulder and above my left breast. Whoever invented this powerport device is a genius! It is helping thousands if not millions of cancer patients around the world.

Second Round of Chemotherapy January 2012

It was now January 2012 and it was snowing pretty badly. It was another Friday and my second round of chemo was ahead of me. The procedure was the same as the first one. There were two nurses. One asked for my name and some personal information. Then I was told the kind of chemotherapy solution I would be receiving carboplatin and paclitaxel. One nurse verified and the other confirmed. This is the first time that the nurses were able to use and access my powerport device. And, it was such a blessing! The experience was so much easier with a powerport. Then they gave me a nice warm blanket and two pillows. Again we were offered snacks, fruit juices and water. I needed to eat and drink something during chemo so I wouldn't get dehydrated. By this time I thought I knew what to expect from the chemo, but I learned that I would have different and more side effects than I already have with my first one.

This was when most of my hair started falling out, something that everyone dreads. I decided to ask my daughter Megan to help me shave off my head.

Since I didn't want to wait until all my hair fell out. I tried not to cry but seeing myself bald for the first time in my life, I was not able to control my tears. It is hard to lose all of your hair at once like that, especially for a woman.

Fatigue also started to set in. I had very limited energy, no appetite and I was easily bruised. I also had low red blood cell counts. I was always tired and sleepy. I felt lightheaded and dizzy a lot. I also lost my appetite but I tried to eat something because I needed to. I was constipated a lot during chemotherapy treatments.

I had my ovarian cancer level and blood tests every week before my chemotherapy treatments. The cancer level and blood tests results are what my oncologist relied on to know my ovarian cancer level (CA125) and if my blood test results are normal and safe for me to have my next chemotherapy treatments or if I need a blood transfusion before chemotherapy.

Remember the CA125 cancer level tests only gauge my ovarian cancer level and not any other cancer. So, for example, if I have brain cancer the CA125 tests will not be able to detect it.

Other tests are used for other types of cancer. Megan was the one who asked Dr. Hantel, MD about this. I was glad she was with me every step of the way, especially when it came to asking the doctors and nurses questions.

Because of my chemo brain, I am not able to remember things that I needed to ask Dr, Hantel, MD.

I learned that before seeing my doctor, I have to write down all the questions I need to ask him because I always forget and in reality he only has about between 10 minutes to 15 minutes to talk to you because he has other patients waiting. Tip: make sure to jot down any questions you have for your doctor too. That way you won't forget the important things that you want to ask them during your appointment.

Blood Transfusion & More Chemo

Another Friday arrived and it brought my third round of chemo. The side effects of chemo got progressively worse each round. On this day, my red blood cell count was so low, that I needed a blood transfusion prior to getting chemo. It took me a while to agree because I was worried that I might get a disease from the blood donor and I didn't want that added to my worries. The nurse assured me that all donor blood is screened and checked for any diseases. I was also told that it will give me more energy. Since I did not have enough energy after my second chemotherapy treatment, I thought that I didn't have anything to lose. I could try and if my body doesn't respond very well to the blood transfusion, then I would ask the nurse to stop the blood transfusion.

This was the first of a few blood transfusions in months to come. I don't like seeing blood in general, especially if it is mine.

So, during the blood transfusion through my powerport, I looked to my right side the whole time to avoid seeing the blood going through my powerport on my left side. Megan joked and said that I was a vampire just taking in my food! Blood transfusions take a long time & it was a very long day for us. A little humor definitely helps you through tough times.

Megan and I were offered free snacks and drinks every time I went in for chemotherapy treatments to hydrate and maintain my blood sugar to normal. I could also use the bathroom which was just outside the room anytime I felt like going to the bathroom by dragging the chemo solution (carboplatin and paclitaxel) with me. The chemotherapy treatments lasted for one hour each session. I could not wait until each of those sessions were over with. I always focused on the finish line and looked forward to when I could go home, take a shower and rest in my own bed in my bedroom. That was my primary focus every single session!

Fourth Round of Chemo

I believe it was still January 2012 and my fourth chemotherapy treatment was up. It was snowing heavily that day too! I had no other choice but to drive because Megan's right ankle sprain was still bothering her. Poor thing! I was more afraid of driving in snow than the actual chemotherapy. Driving while the snow is still falling is very dangerous even if it is just a few miles away since the roads are not plowed yet.

So, it is very slippery and treacherous. We made it to and from the hospital safely, if not a little bit shaken both ways. I always pray every time I drive, especially during the snow.

Driving in the snow has always given me an uncomfortable feeling, but especially after one night when I was driving home from my accounting client's office and I actually landed on a ditch because I drove on a black ice that was covered with fresh snow.

It was dark and the snow was falling heavily. It was difficult to see the road. I surely did not see it. And, I was lucky enough that there were no incoming vehicles and no vehicles behind me at that time. Otherwise, it could have been much worse. At this scary moment, I found out that my little sports car with an all-wheel drive vehicle is just no match for black ice. I learned my lesson the hard way. I only see people landing on a ditch during wintertime on the news on TV but this was me experiencing it first hand. It was terrifying!

After I landed on that ditch and got my composure back, I looked around and it was wide open. It was very dark and so cold. I only got the light from the headlights of my car and from the people driving on the road above me. Then, I started praying to my Mom and Dad to help me get out of that ditch and help me get back on the road. Luckily, I was able to get back on the road. Thank them and thank GOD!

This would be the second to the last entry on my chemotherapy treatments.

Again I had carboplatin and paclitaxel. I would have the same chemotherapy solutions for the rest of the rounds of my chemotherapy for this cancer. I decided not to write the details of every single day of my chemotherapy treatments because it will just be a repetition of the previous treatments and the side effects. I had a total of 18 rounds of chemotherapy treatments for four and a half months, every Friday from December 2011 to April 13, 2012 for my stage 4 aggressive metastatic ovarian cancer. Number 13 is now my lucky number because my last chemotherapy treatment for this ovarian cancer was on April 13, 2012. It was Friday the 13th!

CHAPTER 7: THE WIG

One evening while I was watching TV before I was even diagnosed with my first cancer, a commercial came on about children with cancer needing donated hair in order to make their wigs. I felt so bad for those children. So, I thought this was something that I could do to help out. I grew my hair to almost my hips, much longer than my more normal shoulder-length hair since that was the required length for me to be able to donate my hair. I then had it cut and donated to the children with cancer charity so that they could make a wig from it for them. Less than a year later, I was diagnosed with my first cancer. My right breast cancer. Stage 0. The doctors caught it early enough.

Then a year later my daughter Megan grew her hair really long too and donated it to the children with cancer charity as well. Guess what happened next? I was diagnosed with my 2nd cancer a few months later.

Stage 4 aggressive metastatic ovarian cancer. When I told my oncologist about these weird coincidences, he said you both have good hearts and wanted to help others but stop growing your hair and donating them, in a kind of jokingly but serious way. We followed his advice but I was still diagnosed with my 3rd, 4th, 5th, and 6th cancers after that. Donating our hair to charities to help others, only to then need that same help a few months later were just weird coincidences. But it doesn't make it less weird. From Megan and my good deed to the American Cancer Society's good deed to me.

I didn't lose my hair during my first cancer, since I didn't have chemo, but as I said before, I did lose my hair during my second cancer. Luckily, the American Cancer Society provides free wigs to cancer patients through Edward-Elmhurst Hospital. My niece Marnie gave me a ride and went with me to the special boutique for a wig fitting.

I actually felt lightheaded before Marnie came to my house but I did not tell her about it. I did not want her to worry. I thought this was just one of the side effects of chemo and it will pass and it did.

So, off Marnie and I went to Edward-Elmhurst Hospital in Plainfield, IL. There we met a very nice lady who was in charge of fitting me with a free wig. I wish I could remember her name. She made me feel at ease and not feel sorry for myself. She said that she had helped a lot of cancer patients feel beautiful again by wearing a wig to cover their bald heads. She was kind and compassionate.

It was during this time that she let me choose the wig that I wanted. So, I chose a black shoulder-length wig. Just like the length I normally have my own hair.

She adjusted the wig to the size of my head and I tried it on. Then, she taught me how to wear it without her help. Then she put the wig in a nice box and wished me the best of luck. Marnie and I left soon after that. I think being bald not by choice made me lose my self-confidence for a short while.

Although I never wore the wig again after wearing it at home for practice just for a few minutes, it gave me a sense of confidence that I have the wig to wear just in case I needed it. I said I never wore the wig again because it made my scalp very itchy. And, it made me very uncomfortable thinking that it might just get blown away by the wind when I am outside because I did not have hair for the hair clips to hold onto. The hairnet didn't help either because my entire head felt very itchy every time I tried to clip the wig to the hairnet. I am still grateful though that the American Cancer Society is giving away free wigs to cancer patients. Those wigs are not cheap!

CHAPTER 8: TRIP TO THE ER

There was a day when I did not feel like eating anything but a friend stopped by and gave me a bunch of sweet things from the Philippines to eat. But, that was a big mistake! I forgot that when someone is going through cancer and going through chemotherapy treatments, sugar is a big no. I indulged in those sweets like there was no tomorrow. It was not her fault. I thought since I did not have an appetite, and I haven't had these sweets in many years, maybe eating these delicacies would help me. But I was completely wrong.

My sweet cravings led me to only having a piece of leftover Super Bowl cake for breakfast as well that day. Per usual, Megan made me a fruit smoothie for lunch. I was still working as an accountant during this time. Since I was an independent contractor, I didn't feel comfortable taking a lunch break, so a fruit smoothie was the only thing that I felt like I could eat during lunch without taking a break. I was still able to work that day, but towards the end of the day I felt like I was going to faint.

I was able to drive home but, as soon as I got home, I couldn't breathe. I felt like something heavy was crushing my chest. I was also extremely cold. I asked Megan to take me to the hospital. Since she still couldn't drive because of her sprained ankle, she asked our neighbor to give us a ride instead. I thought this was probably it. I was dying!

We went to the emergency room of Edward-Elmhurst Hospital and waited for a long time. There I was given pills by the emergency doctor to calm me down and to make me feel better. The ER was very busy that day and we spent hours in that room before we could really get a concrete answer about what was wrong with me. This very kind phlebotomist came to draw blood from my veins.

He wasn't certified and trained to take blood from my powerport & wanted to try taking it from my veins first before trying to find a cancer nurse that was certified and trained in powerports. Anxiety immediately washed over me and the fear that I was going to be injured by this procedure made me want to turn him down.

My daughter Megan explained to him my fear and what had happened to me previously when others have tried to draw blood from my arms. He noticed that my daughter was wearing a Celtic cross around her neck & asked if we were Catholic.

We both nodded in agreement and he then said a prayer to the Virgin Mary that he would be able to find my vein right away and cause me no harm. It worked, he was able to find the vein with no problem and draw blood. His kindness and compassion was so appreciated. I'll never forget that!

Shortly after, the ER doctor was finally able to see me. He told me that there was nothing seriously wrong with me and that I wasn't going to die. Essentially, what happened was a combination of my body being weak from the chemo and eating too much sugar in the morning and not enough food during the day.

This caused my blood sugar to crash, which led to a massive anxiety attack. That was why I felt like I couldn't breathe. He told me not to consume a lot of sugar during chemotherapy treatments.

I learned my lesson the hard way. Protein is what I was supposed to eat more of. Of course I knew that! That was one of those things one of the cancer nurses explained to me. But I still ate too much of those sweets that I regret doing. They wanted me to stay overnight at the hospital in order to observe me, just in case. I was transferred to the cancer section of the hospital and my neighbor drove Megan home.

Everyone at the hospital and the cancer section where I stayed overnight were all so kind and compassionate. They gave me something to eat as I have not eaten anything solid since that morning.

I was not able to sleep because the nurses were checking my temperature, blood pressure, etc. every 30 minutes.

Then my oncologist, Dr. Hantel, Md, nurse Sue Budds and my primary doctor, Dr. Weinberg, MD visited me at the hospital early the next morning. While at the hospital, I was able to call Megan before coming to the hospital and my best bud Beth and told them that I was feeling better. Then, I was released from the hospital by my doctors in the afternoon. Megan and my ex-husband Jim came to take me home. At home the first thing I did was to take a shower, wash my hair and wash my clothes.

I really don't like my bedroom bed to smell like a hospital bed. To me hospitals, especially the many hospitals my mom was confined to, smell like medicine. Although my hospital, Edward -Elmhurst Hospital is the cleanest I have been to, it still smells like medicine to me.

CHAPTER 9: THE FALL

In the middle of the night, while still going through chemotherapy, I went to the bathroom around 2:30am and that's all I remembered. It turns out that I fainted outside the bathroom. The left side of my head hit the corner of the wooden entertainment center in the hallway that we were supposed to give away the following morning. Megan was downstairs when she heard the loud bang coming from upstairs where I was. She ran upstairs and found me on the floor with a big red dent on the left side of my head. When she first saw me she thought the worst and thought that I had died because I wasn't moving.

She helped me get up and back into bed. She asked if she should call an ambulance, but I did not bleed and I didn't throw up. I refused to go to the hospital because I was always there every Friday. I thought that I would just wait until then to tell my oncologist about what happened. Megan put me through a few tests to see if I had a concussion and kept me awake for a few hours afterward just in case I did. Everything seemed fine and even though we were shaken up over it, there didn't seem to be anything wrong with me.

Then, Friday came. Megan and I were at the cancer center again for my chemotherapy. I told the nurse what happened and she told my oncologist before I had the chance to tell him myself.

They were both upset and disappointed with me for not calling the hospital. I told them that I was getting tired of being in the hospital all the time. I knew I didn't have a concussion because I didn't throw up and I didn't exhibit any other symptoms.

They were still very concerned that I might have had a concussion. By that time the dent on the left side of my head was so red and very visible without any hair to cover it. A new cancer nurse who didn't know my medical history asked me if I have brain cancer because of the big red dent on my forehead. She thought I just had brain surgery and I was having chemotherapy because of brain cancer. That's how big and visible the dent was!

Also, on that same day, my oncologist found out that my red blood cells count was incredibly low and that was the reason why I fainted. So, another blood transfusion was needed. One thing I learned from chemotherapy is that the doctors will not give it to the patient if the red blood cells count is too low.

A blood transfusion has to be given first in order for chemo to then be administered to the patient.

I learned so many things from my cancer journey and I am thankful to be able to share them with my family, friends, my cancer survivor friends and you.

I am not certain how many times I had blood transfusions during my chemotherapy treatments. There was a time when Megan and I were at the cancer center for my chemotherapy treatment from around 8:00 am to around 7:00 pm because I needed a blood transfusion first. Waiting for the right type of blood from a donor and waiting for my red blood cells count to be normal first after the blood transfusion and before the chemotherapy treatments take a good chunk of time.

It was already dark outside when we left the cancer center but, glad that I was able to have the blood transfusion and chemotherapy that day. Therefore, the number of hours we were there was not completely wasted. We were so happy to be heading back home after 11 hours of being at the hospital. I am so grateful to all of the donors that gave blood to the American Red Cross for me to have those blood transfusions. I am not certain how many blood transfusions I had during my chemotherapy treatments and surgeries but I am so appreciative to all of the kind people who are donating blood to help others. May GOD continue on blessing you all!

CHAPTER 10: MUCH NEEDED DISTRACTIONS

Throughout my entire cancer journey, I was blessed and lucky enough to be surrounded by caring family and friends. It was just a few months after my last chemotherapy was over and I was starting to get back to my normal life. My best bud Beth and her family wanted to treat me to a special day in order to celebrate getting through chemotherapy treatments.

Beth and her husband Kress, along with their kids Ryan, Kendall, and Matt (Kress, Jr) took me to this very nice upscale restaurant in Chicago for dinner, then we went on a horse-driven carriage ride around the Magnificent Mile. They made me feel very important that night. They always do but that night was very special! I didn't expect that I would still be alive because of stage 4 and the size of cancer that I just had.

We also got some popcorn and walked around on a beautiful night in the city of Chicago. It was one of the most amazing and enjoyable nights I spent with them that I will never ever forget for as long as I live!

My cancer journey was not all gloomy and dark because of all of the special people in my life. Exactly 5 months after my last chemotherapy treatments, my hair started to grow back, my energy was almost 100%. Beth and her children took me to Medinah Country Club for dinner to celebrate my birthday. Lucky for me, this was also when the Ryder Cup was being held at Medinah Country Club.

I was not able to attend the actual games because I was trying to avoid being exposed to the big crowd. It was during that time when I was highly susceptible to catching just about anything that would make me sick because my immune system was still very weak. Although Team USA lost to Team Europe, it was an absolute honor for me to be there with my family (Beth and her children Ryan, Kendall, Matt). I enjoyed every minute of that get together with them after what I went through with cancer, chemotherapy and the side effects.

They were all affected by my cancer as well. I could just imagine how they all felt! I know that they all prayed very hard for me. I knew even with their very young age Ryan was around ten years old, Kendall was nine years old and Matt was seven years old, they were all so worried about me.

They constantly told me that they were all praying hard for me and they love me so much. It melts my heart every time I hear them say those words. I love all of them more than they will ever know!

I have known Beth's children since they were born. I actually watched them occasionally when they were growing up. Ryan and Kendall are both now in college and Matt is a junior in high school. Ryan is twenty years old, Kendall is nineteen years old and Matt is seventeen years old. Beth and I have been best friends even before she started having kids. Over twenty-eight years and counting. Beth has a brother but she doesn't have a sister so, I am like the sister that she never had and I am auntie Nora to her children. The special dinner we all got together for my birthday was definitely a celebration for all of us!

It is important for me to say and acknowledge how grateful and thankful I am for Beth, her husband Kress, their children Ryan, Kendall and Matt, and her parents Geri and Norm for everything that they have done for me and Megan. If not for them, especially Geri and Norm, I would not have been able to even see the gate of Medinah Country Club. As an avid golfer, I am so beyond grateful that I was able to play countless rounds of golf at the Medinah Country Club. I was also able to enjoy playing in Ladies tournaments, numerous breakfasts, lunches and dinners for many, many years with them taking me as their guest even before the Ryder Cup.

They have always been there for me before, during and after my cancer. I am truly blessed to have them always on my side all these years. They are all kind, honest, compassionate, caring, and loving human beings that I am very blessed and fortunate to have met and been with. Words are not enough to express how much I appreciate every single thing that they have done for me. Once again they have proven that family is not always blood-related. To be absolutely honest, I am closer to them than most of my blood relatives. I am very proud to call them my family!

CHAPTER 11: FIRST OVARIAN CANCER LAST CHEMO

I t was now a beautiful sunny spring and the last day of my chemotherapy treatments. Needless to say, I was looking forward to this final day. It could not have come soon enough. Thank you, GOD!!!

As soon as we got to the cancer center, Megan and I went straight to the receptionist area to tell them I was already there. After a few minutes of waiting, a nurse called my name and escorted us to the chemotherapy department. Since they were not busy at that moment, the nurse had me choose between a private room or a chair with the other patients facing a man-made pond. I chose a private room. I always choose a private room whenever I have a choice. That way, I can concentrate on praying rather than being distracted outside by a lot of patients.

Some patients are on their phones talking to their loved ones, I hear the sound of the chemotherapy of other patients when it was time for the nurses to turn them off. I hear nurses and other staff walking around and helping other patients. I see patients going in and out of the bathroom. I see others walking to the snack table. I hear nurses talking to each other, etc.

There was no shortage of distractions when you are out in the big room with other patients. That was the reason why if I had a choice between a private room and where all the patients are, I always choose a private room. With the 18 rounds of chemotherapy treatments for this stage 4 aggressive metastatic ovarian cancer, I have been blessed and very lucky that for the most part, I had a private room!

Then two nurses came to the room including the one who had me choose between a private room or a comfortable chair facing a pond. One of the nurses asked me personal and medical questions. Like they always do. They told me the chemotherapy solutions that I was receiving that day were carboplatin and paclitaxel and it will take one hour to get the whole process done with.

The other nurse verified and the other confirmed. I really liked that they do this meticulously to prevent them from making a deadly mistake. Then my powerport was accessed with no problems. So, the last round of chemotherapy solution was administered.

I was so excited waiting for this final day to happen. It was finally happening! It takes one hour for the chemotherapy treatments to be over with.

I was counting the minutes and seconds in my mind the entire time. My red blood was normal that day so I did not need a blood transfusion. Then after eating a few crackers and drinking apple juice and one quick trip to the bathroom, I went back to my room where Megan was waiting for me, closed my eyes and I started praying. One hour passed and I was done with the last of my 18 rounds of chemotherapy treatments. I felt free at last! I said free at last of hopefully cancer, no more coming to the cancer center for chemotherapy treatments, no more side effects and no more blood transfusions. Thank you again and again, my GOD!

The number 13 is now my favorite and lucky number, because my eighteenth rounds of chemotherapy treatments for my stage 4 aggressive metastatic ovarian cancer ended on April 13, 2012. Yes, it was Friday the 13th and my lucky number now!!!

Side Effects of my first 18 Rounds of Chemotherapy treatments

1. Hair loss
2. Fatigue
3. Limited energy
4. No appetite
5. Constipated
6. Nausea
7. Easily bruised
8. Light headed
9. Headaches
10. Sleepless nights
11. Anxiety
12. Tooth loss

CHAPTER 12: FIRED BY ONE OF MY ACCOUNTING CLIENTS

I t was July 2012 at this point and one of my accounting clients of almost 5 years told me that they did not need my services anymore. No reason was given to me but I already knew what the reason was. It was my cancer and ongoing treatments. Although I did not miss any work, I think they were afraid that I would die and would leave them in a limbo with their business accounting. After all, this was my second cancer!

While I certainly understood their decision, it didn't make it any less cruel. The weird part though was they hired someone without letting me know first and they asked me to train her.

If I was a bad person I could have just told them to train her themselves but I maintained my professionalism and trained my job replacement. To say it was an awkward situation for her and me was an understatement. That was that though. After almost five years of being loyal to them and dedicated to my work, I was treated poorly by this company's husband and wife team owners right after one of the most difficult periods of my life. I guess loyalty and hard work do not mean anything to them or compassion for that matter.

This taught me not to tell my prospective accounting clients about my cancer. Because if I learned anything from them, it was the fact that I would be discriminated against by my future accounting clients because of my cancer.

Even though most people in my life were incredibly kind and compassionate to me during my cancer journey, there were others that really didn't care at all about what I was going through. They might have said the right things at times, but words are hollow when your actions say otherwise. That was one of those tough life lessons that I learned back then.

Things did work out in the end because I had found a few more good accounting clients after them. Life's good! I was very happy with my new accounting clients. I would say that in a way it was a blessing in disguise that I was fired by one of my oldest clients. Because my new clients were all nice and true professionals.

I did not tell any of them that I had cancer because if I could function 100% with my work as an accountant then, there was no need for them to know and worry or possibly drop me with no warning.

I thought if I had another cancer and I would not be able to work then, that was the time for me to tell them. I was able to work with them for a while and fulfilled my obligation to them. When yet another cancer came later, I was really sad to tell them that I would not be able to continue working with them or working at all.

They were all very kind and understanding and even wished me the best of luck. I referred some of them to my friend and tax accountant, Susan Lewis, CPA. May GOD continue blessing all of them!

CHAPTER 13: ANOTHER CANCER DIAGNOSIS LEFT BREAST CANCER

I t was late 2013, and after another mammogram, MRI, left breast ultrasound, left breast needle biopsy, I was diagnosed with my third cancer in my left breast. When I learned about this cancer, I was not as worried as the first and second cancers. This left breast cancer was stage 0 like my right breast cancer. Somehow I managed to keep my composure and not get emotional as the first two. I thought to myself if I survived the first two then I would survive this one as well. I was just going with the flow at this time.

When my oncologist, Dr. Hantel, MD told me about the results, I did not see him worried so, I did not worry either. Instead, I just paid attention and followed his recommendations. I trust Dr. Hantel completely!

It was time to schedule another surgery. I had a different breast cancer surgeon than my right breast surgery. He was recommended to me by Dr. Hantel, my ovarian cancer oncologist. This time it was the head breast cancer surgeon, Dr. Montana, MD of Dupage Medical Group. The surgery was done at the same hospital, Edward-Elmhurst Hospital. He removed more than the size of my cancer so I did not have to go through another chemotherapy or radiation.

Also, he left color coded clips where the cancer was removed in my left breast. I guess for future reference when the cancer comes back. Although both of my breasts are now hollow, I feel truly blessed that I still have both of my breasts. I actually haven't worn a bra since I had two cancers on my right side, right neck lymph nodes, and above my right shoulder blade and my powerport is below my left shoulder and above my left breast. Wearing a bra aggravates those areas so, I have been wearing strapless shirts under my clothes. I also have a powerport pillow or commonly known as a port pillow to protect my powerport when I am driving or just a passenger in the car.

In one of my follow-up mammograms and appointment with Dr. Montana, he asked me who performed my right breast lumpectomy surgery. I thought that he was the one that did since I already had many doctors and surgeons at that time.

He said that I did not have his signature incision. I never knew until that day that surgeons have their own signature incisions. We later found out that my right breast surgeon was one of the surgeons under him.

Dr. Montana was correct that my left breast surgical scar is nice, straight and clean because he was the one that operated on my left breast. Whereas, my right breast is not. I think it was because the first surgeon opened me up twice in the same incision less than two weeks apart because she was not able to remove all the cancer the first time. I am not going to mention my right breast surgeon's name here as I am still questioning in my mind why she failed to remove the cancer sample she needed from the first surgery. It would have saved me from going under the knife twice.

The fact that I had surgery on the same breast twice in two weeks created a not so smooth surgical scar. The first breast cancer surgeon also left color coded clips where the cancer was removed in my right breast. Therefore, when I have mammograms, my both breasts light up because of the colored clips in both my breasts. This makes it a lot easier for the breast radiologists to see and read my mammogram results.

I did not go through another chemo or radiation for my left breast cancer. It was stage 0. Just like my right breast cancer stage 0. But, my breast cancer doctor/surgeon, Dr. Montana, MD suggested that I might want to have a mastectomy on both breasts so that the cancer will not come back. This would also mean that I wouldn't have to deal with painful mammograms and MRIs, etc. anymore.

I followed his advice and met with a breast reconstructive surgeon, Dr. Ferlmann, MD. He was a down to earth kind of doctor/surgeon. He explained to me the procedure, the recovery time, etc. He also said that the reconstructive surgery will be performed right after the mastectomy surgery the same day and at the Edward-Elmhurst Hospital. He took pictures of my breasts and gave me some time to think about it. After that consultation, I went home and thought about it.

I called Dr. Montana, MD, my left breast cancer surgeon the following day and I told him that I will hold off on the mastectomy surgery for both my breasts. I said that when the cancer comes back, then I would go through with a mastectomy, but not until then. Then I called the breast reconstructive surgeon, Dr. Ferlmann, MD, and told him that I decided to wait. He suggested that I keep his phone number handy just in case I needed to call him to proceed with the reconstructive surgery. I said yes and thank you. I treasure the years that I still have both of my breasts.

The mastectomy procedure reminded me of my sister Tess' own mastectomy surgery. She lost one of her breasts. She never wanted to have reconstructive surgery after mastectomy so she just stuffed her bra with a scarf when she was still alive. She was comfortable that way instead of going through reconstructive surgery. She actually made fun of herself from time to time by saying when the weather was too hot, she just pulled the scarf from her bra and used it as a tissue to wipe off her face and then put the scarf back in her bra when she didn't need it anymore. I believe she purposely did that so we did not have to feel sorry for her.

My sister Tess' mastectomy surgery did not influence my decision at all to not have my own mastectomy. But when my breast cancer comes back, I would be the first one to say let's get rid of both my breasts but not until then!

I continued to take the prescription medications that my oncologist prescribed. Some have given me bad side effects like constipation, nausea, lightheadedness, headaches, fatigue. I really could not wait until I am not taking any more medication but that would be impossible. I take cholesterol, vitamin d3, calcium and Tylenol for pain but this is my life now. I currently have that seven-day pill holder Megan bought for me so I don't forget to take my daily medications. It seemed like it was not too long ago when I bought my mom the same kind of pill holder. My mom has been gone for over eighteen years now. Time flies!

I remember reminding my mom constantly to take her vitamins and other medications when she was still alive. Now it is my daughter, Megan reminding me not to forget to take my medications. It's the circle of life, I guess!

CHAPTER 14: THE RETURN OF MY OVARIAN CANCER

I continued to go to the cancer center in order to have my ovarian cancer level tested on a regular basis. That was when my fourth cancer was detected. I am so thankful for those regular ovarian cancer level tests, because without them catching my cancer early, I would have not survived cancer. Even though there are times when I literally dragged my feet in going to the cancer center, I still managed to be there on time because I know that it is for my own good.

I was always praying and hoping that my ovarian cancer level test results are low if not the lowest and my blood test results are normal, and the nurse assigned to me that particular day would be able to access my powerport easily with no problems, etc. Yet, there I was with yet another cancer. Another challenge for me to overcome.

It seemed like most of my cancer was diagnosed before Thanksgiving and this was no exception, it is now November 2014. Prior to the appointment, I had felt a lump in the base of my right neck. So, I made sure to mention this to my oncologist during my regular appointment with him. I still remember the look on his face when he felt the lump. I told him that I was very concerned and he replied that he was also very concerned. He ordered more tests to see what that lump was.

I went in for an ultrasound and needle biopsy of my right neck at the Edward-Elmhurst Hospital. The ultrasound was a breeze but the needle biopsy not so much. 1% Lidocaine was used locally. Then A 17 gauge guiding needle was used under real time ultrasound. I know Lidocaine local anesthesia was administered but I still felt every centimeter of that long needle go in my neck. The conclusion was it was an enlarged right supraclavicular lymph node 18x24 mm in size. Then a sample of the mass was taken and a needle biopsy clip was left in my right side of the neck for the doctors to see where the cancer was located. Then the mass sample was sent to the laboratory for analysis. Megan and I anxiously waited for the results.

To this day I can still remember how long the needle was and how I felt it going through my right neck. Every time I think of that day, I actually rub my neck where the cancer was. Guess what? I am actually rubbing the right side of my neck while writing this section. Haha!

My right neck lymph nodes needle biopsy results were in. My ovarian cancer oncologist, Dr. Alexander Hantel called me and told me to come to the cancer center to discuss the results. I knew something was wrong because my oncologist only calls me directly when I have another cancer. Otherwise, it will be his nurse, Maria, calling me or it will just be on mychart for me to read.

So, off I went alone and saw my oncologist again. I figured this is just another bump in the road for me. I can handle it. As soon as the door opened, my oncologist came in and told me it was another cancer. Even though I felt like I was prepared for the news, I still felt like my jaw just dropped and my heart came out of my chest.

I saw his facial reaction that I had never seen before. I asked him if he was worried and he said, "yes I am worried but I will do everything I can for you to live longer".

We discussed what to do next. I found out that I would not be able to have the same type of radiation that I had before on that side of my body because I already had radiation on my right breast years prior. By the way, this right neck lymph node cancer was stage 4.

He told me that this cancer was inoperable due to its location. He recommended for me to see my breast cancer radiologist, Dr.Neil Das Gupta, MD who also happened to be the head of the radiology department of the cancer center. I tried to keep my emotions intact while I was talking to Dr. Hantel and could not wait until I was out of his office. All I thought about was to be strong and remain positive for my daughter Megan.

At the same time another cancer diagnosis is something that I could not fathom!

On my way out of the cancer center building this very nice and compassionate social worker, Sharon, seemed to be always there every time I was diagnosed with another cancer. She led me to her office and I just started to cry my heart out again. She knew that I had another cancer to deal with and this time it might be the cancer that would end my life. I told her that this one was in my right neck lymph nodes, stage 4 and it is inoperable. And, this was my fourth cancer.

She knew about my stage 4 ovarian cancer and the other cancer as well. She was always there for moral support for both Megan and myself. Megan and I appreciate her very much!

I saw and felt the sadness on her face. I thought to myself, this is a job that I would not have been able to handle. I know that I was not the first and last patient she has seen so emotionally affected in her entire career. Let alone, the patients that she had seen suffer and die.

She retired a few years ago. I am sad that I do not see her at the cancer center anymore, but I am very happy for her that she gets to be with her daughter and husband and just relax and enjoy her retirement. I consider her my friend. I hope that she is enjoying her retirement and doing well in life!

CHAPTER 15: CYBERKNIFE RADIATION THERAPY

I went and saw my breast cancer radiologist, Dr. Das Gupta, MD and we discussed the treatment that I needed to once again kill this new cancer. Since radiation and surgery were both out of the question, he recommended cyberknife radiation therapy. He said that cyberknife is a robot that is only used for head and neck cancers that are inoperable.

Since then, I have read that it is now used for other parts of the body in addition to head and neck cancers as well. He said that the cyberknife robot was non-surgical and very precise in targeting the cancer itself.

The cyberknife robot is guided by sophisticated software and advanced imaging. It tracks the cancer, as well as the patient's movement while delivering beams of high-dose radiation with a high percentage of accuracy. It also allows the doctors to zero in on the cancer without damaging the good and surrounding healthy cells.

He told me, "if the cyberknife works, my right neck lymph nodes cancer will be totally eradicated by this robot".

I thought that this robot sounded like a miracle and hoped that it would work to kill off my cancer. I will enthusiastically try it out.

Since the cyberknife robot is literally a multi-million dollar machine, Edward-Elmhurst Hospital did not have it here in the Naperville location yet. So, I needed to drive all the way to another town but it is still part of Edward-Elmhurst hospital. It was a three-day session, every other day.

The first day of my cyberknife radiation therapy was in December 2014. I was both excited and anxious to get this done right away. The first hour was spent explaining to me what the process will be like by the cancer nurse. I remember her telling me that both my feet will be bound and my arms will be tied on the sides of the bed so I will be in the same position while having the cyberknife radiation therapy.

She said this is a very sensitive machine and I should not move because if I did then they would have to repeat the process all over again.

Repeating the process was not something that I would want to do. I have been through a lot already with my cancer journey so my answer is heck no, I will not move if that's all it takes!

I believe that I have been a very good listener and a very obedient patient all throughout my cancer journey. I just follow everything my doctors and their medical team tell me what to do. So, I began my first cyberknife radiation therapy. The robot focuses on killing the cancer. The bad cells instead of the good and healthy cells. This machine is precise in targeting the cancer itself. There were always two nice and helpful technicians one male and the other female outside the room divided by glass window in this extremely clean big room, a bed where I was supposed to lay on, a huge cyberknife robot, a nice lighted tropical tree picture above to focus on while I am having the therapy treatments.

There was even nice music that I got to choose from myself. The therapy sessions were from thirty to forty-five minutes each session. Like what the cancer nurse said, my feet were bound and my arms were tied to the sides of the bed. The first day was good. There weren't any problems. I just focused on that nice lighted tropical picture on the ceiling and sometimes closed my eyes while listening to the music. I was disciplined. I did not move and I just kept praying for me to get through this session. And, thank GOD I did!

Next up was my second cyberknife radiation therapy session. The same nice and kind two technicians a male and a female were there. Again everything went as smoothly as possible. The cyberknife robot did its job. By this time I could not wait until the last session was done and over with.

Same as the last time, I closed my eyes while listening to the music and I just kept praying until it was over. The cyberknife radiation delivers beams of high-dose radiation that the sessions are divided into three sessions. They were twice the first week and the last one was the second week.

The side effects were tolerable. I experienced fatigue, always sleeping, and not much of an appetite. There is no comparison to the chemotherapy side effects that I went through in 2011 and 2012. Because of the high-dose radiation that I had, my whole body was probably glowing the entire time. Haha!

My third and my last cyberknife radiation therapy session finally came. I was looking forward to this last session. So, I had my usual smiley face and positive attitude going into the therapy room. The two nice and compassionate technicians were there to welcome me again. I wished that I could remember their names so I could mention and thank them here in my book. But, my chemo brain wouldn't let me remember.

I knew the drill at this time. Remove my shoes, and no jewelry, wear my hospital gown and lay on my back, my feet were bound, and my arms were tied to the sides of the bed. I was pretty confident and really excited to get this last cyberknife radiation therapy over with.

The technicians asked if I was ready. And, ready I was! So, the cyberknife robot like the first two sessions moved and focused on my right side of the neck. With my eyes closed, I was in the same position listening to the music and praying at the same time when I heard a loud squeaky sound coming from the robot that I did not hear in the first and second sessions.

With my eyes still closed I started to wonder what that loud sound was. Maybe, it was a computer glitch from where the technicians were or something else? A million things were going through my mind at that time. I did not know what to think anymore. I was getting restless. But, I couldn't move because my feet were bound and my hands were tied to the sides of the bed. Also, I didn't want the whole process to be done all over again.

At one point, I stopped praying and opened my eyes. I saw the male technician running towards me and he tried to stop the robot by placing his arms in between the robot and my body. I asked him what was happening. He said **"the robot malfunctioned and he was afraid that it might crush me"**. Oh my goodness!

That was a very scary moment. What else could go wrong? Here I thought maybe, this happened to another patient before and they know what to do.

I probably was overthinking at that point. But, I was relieved and grateful to him that his quick reaction saved me from getting hurt.

Remember my feet were bound and my arms were tied on the sides of the bed? So, I was not able to move.

He said, **"don't you worry, I just unplugged the robot and they called the repairman."** I asked how long will the repairman take to fix it.

He replied that the repairman was in the building and will just take him a few minutes to fix the robot. Thankfully, the robot was fixed, but it took me over an hour instead of forty-five minutes to get this last session done. I was not complaining though. At least I did not get crushed when the robot malfunctioned! I'm so thankful for that technician who was fast enough to save me. My third and final cyberknife radiation therapy was now done and over with. That's another procedure done and in the books. Thank GOD!

Now, I had to wait a few months for the results to find out if the cyberknife radiation therapy really worked for me. If it did, it would eradicate my right neck lymph nodes from stage 4 cancer completely.

Meanwhile, while waiting for the results, I was still going through ovarian cancer level tests, blood tests, mammograms, MRI, pet scans, thyroid scans, bone density scans, EKG, and other procedures.

The cyberknife radiation therapy 3 sessions 2014 side effects were tolerable to me:

1. I had a hard time sleeping
2. Not much of an appetite
3. Fatigue

I was probably glowing in the dark due to the high dosage of radiation during the therapy sessions. Just kidding!

After a few months of waiting, the time had come for the big results of my cyberknife radiation therapy. It was now 2015. I was at the cancer center patiently and anxiously waiting for my breast cancer oncologist, Dr. Das Gupta, MD, to tell me if the cyberknife worked. **He told me the great news that my stage 4 inoperable right neck lymph node cancer was completely eradicated by the cyberknife robot machine!** Tears of joy were rolling down my face. I can't remember the number of times I thanked Dr. Das Gupta at that moment. Needless to say, I was relieved and very happy. Thank GOD again! Another prayer was answered.

Then I went upstairs on the second floor to see my regular ovarian cancer oncologist, Dr. Hantel and he too gave me the great news and confirmed that my right neck lymph nodes cancer was completely eradicated by the cyberknife robot! I was now cancer free again. But Dr. Hantel said that I am in remission for my ovarian cancer for now. Because of the kind of cancer that I have, stage 4 aggressive metastatic ovarian cancer, he specifically said that my cancer will come back.

We just don't know when and which part of my body is next. So, I was not out of the woods yet. I was in remission from my fourth cancer but not cancer free yet. That's what I like about Dr. Hantel. He is honest, will tell you the truth, and not sugarcoat anything! I am thankful and I appreciate him for that.

CHAPTER 16: ORAL CHEMOTHERAPY LYNPARZA

I t was still 2015. After my follow-up mammogram, ductal carcinoma in situ (the presence of abnormal cells inside a milk duct in the breast) was found in my left breast. So, I was put on oral chemo called Lynparza tablets 500mg. These tablets are like horse pills. They are big and I took 8 tablets in the morning and 8 tablets at night, a total of 16 tablets a day.

I was also prescribed Arimidex tablets 1mg a day. So, with my lovastatin 20mg (1) for cholesterol, vitamin d3 (2), and extra strength Tylenol (2), I was taking 22 pills a day. I took Lynparza tablets for oral chemotherapy for 14 days. On the fourteenth day, I started having a hard time swallowing the 16 tablets a day. That was enough for me. I asked Dr. Hantel, MD if I could stop taking them because I was having a difficult time swallowing those big pills, terrible side effects like nauseated a lot, lightheadedness, headaches, and easily bruised. So, with Dr. Hantel's go signal, I stopped taking Lynparza immediately but I was still taking Arimidex 1mg tablets a day.

This was the worst up until that time because I forced myself to take all those tablets 8 tablets at a time twice a day for 14 days. The tablets were like the size of horse pills.

Oral Chemotherapy Lynparza's side effects on me:

1. I felt like my throat was closing up. I had a hard time swallowing the tablets that were the size of horse pills
2. Headaches
3. Lightheadedness
4. Nauseated
5. Easily bruised
6. Constipated

CHAPTER 17: PROGRAMS: WHY WEIGHT AND BACK ON TRACK

As soon as my oral chemotherapy was over. I needed to get back to my normal life. I started asking around what kind of programs I can join at the cancer center & Sharon, one of the hospital's social workers, was able to steer me in the right direction. So, I joined a couple of free programs offered to cancer patients. I am so glad that I did because I met some amazing and incredible people! Without these programs, I would have never met them.

From September 16, 2015 to December 9, 2015, I participated in the "Why Weight" program at the Edward-Elmhurst Hospital cancer center taught by Ms.Doreen Berard. It was a big class. There were probably 8 to 10 cancer patients in that program. Before every class started, we were weighed and recorded by Doreen. I think it is the weighing part of the program that some of the cancer patients do not like. The rest of the program was really interesting from meditation, yoga, etc.

I learned portion-controlled meals which include protein, carbs, fruits and vegetables. Drink plenty of water. Avoid drinking sodas. Eat 5 times a day including snacks in between lunch and dinner, writing down what we ate and showing her what we ate. I actually bought a food scale to weigh my food intake. I also learned the importance of yoga and meditation. This class was very helpful to me as I started gaining weight before taking this class. Then I lost some weight because of this class and with the help of the Back on Track workout program for cancer patients. My full explanation is below.

I also joined the "Back on Track" workout program.

This fitness program is led by abled and well-trained physical trainers Britt and Brooke (whom I consider my friends) for cancer patients who were recovering from cancer or cancer caregivers at the Edward-Elmhurst Hospital Health Center.

I enjoyed both programs where I learned about eating the right kind of food, counted calorie intake, walked 4 miles a week, and did the exercises that I wanted and needed. I was able to lose some weight, felt rejuvenated and most of all I was able to be with cancer patients like me. We listened to each other's stories and told our own cancer experiences. Although we had different cancers, the pain and sufferings are the same. We even went out to lunch a few times. It was like a breath of fresh air! I could finally feel and see that my life was starting to feel normal again.

I learned that one can not lose weight without taking both programs at the same time. Because of that, both Why Weight and Back on Track programs go hand in hand. The sad and devastating part was that sometimes you would find out that the person that was usually next to you in the program was not coming back because they died the night before. Those people who died have plans for dinner with their families. We really do not know when our last time here on earth would be. Let's all enjoy our lives to the fullest one day at a time. And, don't forget to say you love someone before it's too late!

I have ended up outliving healthy people that did not show any health problems at all the last few years, even people who were not a part of the cancer programs. Since my cancer journey started, I have lost two of my siblings. My older sister Tess died unexpectedly of a heart attack and stroke while spending a long weekend trip with her friends in 2018.

She was 67 years old. She left her family and home without knowing that she would be back home in ashes.

As I write this, my brother Rico died unexpectedly just a few days ago. He just turned 69 years old. Sometimes I feel guilty that they are both gone. Tess and Rico were a big part of my prayer warriors! And now, they are both gone!

I also learned to accept that death does not discriminate. It will end your life when your time is up no matter what and no matter who you are! Please feel free to give your loved ones big hugs and tell them you love them!

CHAPTER 18: BEING DECLARED DISABLED

I n March 2015, I was declared disabled because of my stage 4 aggressive metastatic ovarian cancer and the side effects of my first 18 rounds of chemotherapy. This meant that I was now eligible and approved for social security disability and medicare benefits. My friend, Sharon (former social worker) at the Edward-Elmhurst Hospital gave me the name of the hospital representative who could help me apply for social security disability and medicare health insurance. I called, set up an appointment and went straight to the hospital with all the documents I needed and applied.

The hospital representative told me that it would take probably three months for us to hear from social security.

He would call me when that happens. Well, my application was approved within just a few days! The hospital representative said that he has not seen anything like this before and it usually takes at least three months. I was very surprised to get a call from social security within just a few days telling me that my application was approved. I was actually so shocked! I actually asked the social security person if they were able to talk to all my doctors and oncologists in such a short time already about my medical history. She said no they don't call doctors but they rely and trust on the hospital's patient's medical record which they obtained from Edward -Elmhurst Hospital immediately. It was then read and analyzed by their own medical team. She also said that because I had stage 4 aggressive metastatic ovarian cancer that started in 2011 that I was already eligible to apply in 2012. Since I did not apply until 2015, they can only give me benefits starting 2014. They can only go one year after filing an application and approval. Oh, I just wish I knew. Still a huge Blessing, though! Thank you, GOD!

I am so thankful that Edward-Elmhurst Hospital had a representative that could help me through the process. I have heard and read stories about people trying to navigate getting approved for disability benefits on their own and how hard of a time they had. It was such a blessing to work with someone that knew exactly what to do in order for me to get the help that I needed.

The hospital's charity foundation also helped me for years by paying my hospital bills during my cancer journey. Whatever my Medicare health insurance did not cover, the hospital covered. So I was able to concentrate on getting better and not worrying about paying my hospital bills. Thank GOD for them.

I was happy and sad at the same time about being approved for social security benefits and medicare benefits. Happy, because I do not have to worry about not being able to work to make a living when I could no longer physically and mentally do so, but sad that I would not be able to go back to work because I am not the same person anymore. It is difficult for me to comprehend and remember things now because of my chemo brain. So, there was no way to do accounting work because in accounting, it is the detail and accuracy that matters. Although my monthly income is not the same as it was when I was working, it is still a big help financially. In a way it is like a forced retirement that was beyond my control. I miss most of my accounting clients. I hope that they are all doing well in life both personally and professionally.

Then when I turned 66 years old my disability benefits were automatically converted to regular social security retirement benefits. It is important to note that social security and medicare benefits are not charity. Our contributions to these programs were deducted from our payroll income during our working years. I worked for well over 44 years and I earned every single penny of what I am receiving today.

CHAPTER 19: FAMILY VISITS FROM THE PHILIPPINES

I n March 2015, my sisters Tess, Lynne, niece Shelly, and nephew Rafael came all the way from the Philippines to visit me and Megan.

It was an exciting, happy and emotional visit from them. Megan and I have not seen them in many years.

It was also the last time I saw my sister Tess alive. They stayed in Illinois for just a few days because they were visiting other relatives and friends in different states as well. Megan and I were able to do things with them for a few hours. We went shopping, had lunch at Portillo's, showed them the Naperville Riverwalk, just stayed home, had dinner and talked for the most part.

I could tell that my sister Tess was physically tired because she fell asleep on the couch while the kids and Lynne were playing outside with the leftover snow. They were very excited and had a great time seeing snow for the first time in their lives. They were able to experience making a snowman and snow angels. We took lots of pictures to be shared on social media, of course! Then the following day we took them to Oak Brook Mall for a little shopping. I just wished I knew that my sister Tess was going to die three years later. Those were incredibly precious hours we all got to share with each other and be together. Good times!

It was also during this time 2015 when they were still here that I was approved for social security disability and medicare benefits. They were all so happy for me. Not knowing that I was already qualified for social security disability and medicare benefits in 2012 when I had my second cancer stage 4 aggressive metastatic ovarian cancer in 2011. Had I known that then I would have saved one of my former accounting clients from firing me in 2012, just three months after my chemotherapy treatments were over.

But I would not have been able to meet and help my other nice and professional accounting clients.

I believe that everything happens for a reason. In my own personal experiences, the reason is always to my favor. I am not going to get tired of saying that I am Blessed and lucky again and again!!!

CHAPTER 20: CANCER RETURNS AGAIN 5TH CANCER

Because of my regular ovarian cancer level tests, blood tests, PET scan, other procedures, and follow-ups with my oncologist, Dr. Hantel, MD. He found another cancer during late 2015. It was then when I was diagnosed with yet another cancer next to my left rib cage. This was my fifth cancer. I thought my cancer left my body completely by now but apparently not!

Now, I fully understand why Dr. Hantel, MD said that I am in remission for my 4th neck lymph nodes inoperable cancer instead of saying I am cancer free.

There was a reason why my cancer is classified as stage 4 aggressive metastatic ovarian cancer because cancer jumps from one part of my body to another. My cancer just kept jumping and coming back!

Again, we discussed what to do next. Since my ovarian cancer responded very well to my first rounds of chemotherapy in 2011, he recommended that I go through another rounds of chemotherapy treatments. I asked if we can wait until sometime in March when the snow will not be as heavy to start with the chemotherapy treatments, because I did not want to drive in the snow again like last time. I am scared of driving in snow when the snow is actually falling when I am driving. I said if it can wait I would rather wait. He said not to wait very long because my cancer is aggressive. I said I understand. He then agreed.

So, March 2016 was the agreed month that I should start to have my chemotherapy treatments again. Remember I already have 18 rounds of chemo for my stage 4 ovarian cancer in 2011 to 2012. Then 14 days of oral chemo. Now this...

CHAPTER 21: AND IT RETURNED AGAIN

While waiting for March 2016 to start chemotherapy for my cancer on the left side next to the rib cage, I was diagnosed with my sixth cancer in January 2016. It was the result of my regular ovarian cancer level, blood tests, PET scan, etc. The cancer was lymph nodes above my right shoulder blade.

Now, the chemotherapy to kill my fifth cancer left side next to my rib cage would now kill the sixth cancer above my right shoulder blade as well. I think the couple of months we waited for the chemotherapy to start was a blessing in disguise.

Whereas, if I had the chemotherapy right away for my 5th cancer, this sixth cancer would not have been detected.

Instead, it would just be killed with the chemotherapy without us knowing. Either way I was glad that they were both detected early enough and eradicated. I am counting my blessings! Thank you, GOD, again and again!

CHAPTER 22: CHEMOTHERAPY FOR CANCER #5 AND CANCER #6

Here we go again! My first chemotherapy for these cancers started on March 4, 2016 and ended on June 28, 2016. Like my chemo in 2011-2012, Megan and I were at the cancer center of Edward -Elmhurst Hospital. We went directly to the receptionist area to let them know that I was already there. Then a nurse came and took Megan and I to the chemotherapy department. There, I was asked for my name, date of birth and some personal information. The usual important stuff. Then I was asked if I wanted a private room or a chair with the other patients facing a man-made pond. I chose a private room so I can concentrate on praying.

I always choose a private room whenever I have a choice. Another nurse came into the room and explained how the chemotherapy works. We were offered snacks and drinks. And, the bathroom was just outside the room where I was in case I needed to use the bathroom. Now there were two nurses in the room with me and Megan.

I was told PARP inhibitors, Doxil and carboplatin will be the chemotherapy solutions I will be receiving. It will take one hour for the chemotherapy to be done and over with. Then one nurse verified and the other nurse confirmed my information and the kind of chemotherapy solution I will have. I like that the nurses were very thorough to avoid potential deadly mistakes. Then they accessed my powerport with no problems and the chemotherapy started. I closed my eyes and prayed. I had crackers and apple juice so I didn't get dehydrated. I also used the bathroom once by dragging the chemotherapy stand with me. Then the first chemo was over and in the books.

My second chemotherapy was up. It was now May 3, 2016. I don't remember why I didn't have chemotherapy in April but I had two in May. The procedure was the same and I had the same chemotherapy solutions, PARP inhibitors, Doxil, and carboplatin. I did not have a private room this time because they were very busy. I was in the big room with the other patients facing a man-made pond. Again, we were offered snacks and fruit juices, and water. I had my usual crackers and apple juice and I used the bathroom once.

I closed my eyes again and prayed. My cancer survivor friends Wendy and Terri visited me at the cancer center while I was having chemo. I was surprised to see them. I did not even think that we could accept visitors but the staff at the cancer center let them in. I appreciate them for visiting me because it took my mind off the chemotherapy treatment. Then one hour passed and I was done with my second chemo. Very happy to leave the cancer center and go straight home.

We used to go out to lunch with our friend Harold who is also a cancer survivor but because of the pandemic, we really have not seen each other. Also, I heard that Terri moved to Florida recently. Wendy and I text each other once in a while. Also, we see each other's posts on social media. Thank you, ladies and

Harold. I hope that you are all doing well. I can not wait for our next get-together. So many things to catch up on. Stay healthy and safe always my friends!

My third chemotherapy. It was now May 31, 2016. Again, Megan and I were at the cancer center. They were very busy that day. I was given a reclining chair facing a man-made pond with some of the cancer patients. The nurses asked for my personal information and told me that PARP inhibitors, Doxil, and carboplatin are the chemotherapy solutions I was receiving today. Then one nurse verified and the other nurse confirmed. Even though I was with the other patients, it felt so serene and peaceful just looking at the pond.

While I was looking at the pond, a cardinal bird showed up on the glass window. We were on the second floor. Megan witnessed the whole thing. I always believe that when you see a cardinal, a loved one is visiting you. I knew it was my mom telling me that I will be alright. The cardinal bird was just there not moving and just staring at me for a few minutes. Megan and I looked at each other. I couldn't believe it was just there without moving. I smiled and I talked to my mom silently telling her that I love her and not to worry about me. Then, the cardinal bird flew away.

This was now June 28, 2016. My fourth and last chemotherapy. The procedure was the same. Since they were not busy, I chose a private room. There were two nurses. One nurse asked for my personal information like they always do. I was told that PARP inhibitors, Doxil, and carboplatin were the chemotherapy solutions I will be receiving today. One nurse verified and the other nurse confirmed. This was also the day when I asked my oncologist, Dr. Hantel, MD if I can stop the chemo after this. I had so many side effects including tongue thrust with this chemo. I didn't lose my hair with that chemo, though, which was a plus. That was a good thing. I will write about all the side effects later.

I started with my chemotherapy for both my 5th and 6th

cancers once a month every Friday in March 2016 and ended in June 2016. Two months earlier than the scheduled treatment end time. I can tell you that this chemotherapy was very strong and undeniably had the worst side effects on me.

Which was the reason why I asked Dr. Hantel to stop the chemotherapy treatments after 4 months. I told him and my daughter, Megan, that I could not handle any more side effects of the chemotherapy treatments. I learned later that it was the PARP inhibitors and Doxil that my body did not tolerate well. If by stopping the treatments, I will lose my life, then so be it. I was at peace with that and I didn't want to continue with chemotherapy treatments anymore and continue to experience the terrible side effects.

At this point, I realized why some cancer patients would rather die than go through the awful side effects of chemo. Remember this was the third time that I went through chemo. I survived the first one with 18 rounds, the second with 14 days of oral chemo and this third one was 4 rounds instead of 6 rounds. A total of 36 rounds. And, all have given me terrible side effects, especially these last rounds:

I developed thrush in my tongue, mouth and esophagus in April 2016 while I was on chemotherapy treatment. It was painful and hard to swallow. I lost my appetite. I was given stronger prescription oral medication to get rid of it because the over the counter medication did not work. Thankfully, the prescription medication worked after a few days. I was also given medication for anxiety and nausea. I was never anxious in my whole life before.

I developed neuropathy in both my hands and feet. Which is the reason why I now walk with a cane on long walks. My pink cane, which inspired the name of this book.

Neuropathy has also made holding on to things very difficult. I often drop things without having any control over them.

I now have chemo brain. It is difficult for me to remember things and words to say. I could not engage intelligently with someone because I forget the words to say as I was saying them. Sometimes I come up with words to describe what I am thinking of saying and other times I can't come up with anything. I know that this can be frustrating and annoying sometimes when conversing with me for my daughter and others, but that's the way it is now for me.

I am thankful and grateful that I can still do most of the things on my own but at a slower pace now unlike before when I could multitask.

I could not lift heavy things anymore. I drop things not on purpose but because I could not control my hands. I have constant pain in my right arm, right breast and right armpit because of lymphedema caused by lymph nodes removal in my right armpit. I live with it now.

I was nauseated and exhausted all the time and sometimes I still am. I have constant body aches and pains.

I developed eczema below both my eyebrows and outside both of my ears a few days after the 2nd chemotherapy treatment. I still suffer from it to this day.

Once I had my appetite back, I started gaining so much weight because of no exercise.

My cholesterol was elevated and I am now borderline diabetic. I stopped drinking soda over 4 months ago and I only lost 5 lbs. At least I have not gained that 5 lbs back. Still not good enough!

I can not stay focused and concentrate on something. Watching 2 hours of movies on TV is a little challenging to say the least. I now always have to watch the same show twice and take breaks in between for me to understand the story. I was not like this before chemotherapy.

I lost two teeth luckily they were both in the back of my mouth. I feel like my teeth are now weak. I try not to eat hard food.

I told my daughter Megan that I am not as smart as I used to be. This is not a joke and I am really serious here. I used to be able to engage and participate in a healthy intelligent conversation with anybody. For example, I'll end up saying "anybody" when I mean to say, "anymore" when I am forgetting the words to say. It is incredibly disappointing and frustrating. I have the chemotherapy side effects to blame for that. Some days are better than others.

I still recommend chemotherapy to cancer patients, though! But, despite all the side effects which I will probably have for the rest of my life, I should not be complaining because I am still alive because the chemotherapy treatments worked for me after all.

Remember I am BRCA2 positive? This means that my ovarian cancer responds very well to chemotherapy treatments. Compared to BRCA1-positive patients. Also, my BRCA2 gene is fighting cancer itself per my oncologist, Dr. Hantel, MD. I should always remember to be thankful and grateful for this blessing! And, I certainly am!!

CHAPTER 23: RING THE CANCER BELL

My last chemotherapy treatment was on June 28, 2016. This was the day when I was finally able to ring the cancer bell since I was done with my chemotherapy treatments. I didn't get to do this with my previous cancers because the hospital did not have a cancer bell yet. I got so emotional with my daughter Megan and some of the nurses that were there during all my 6 cancers. They were all so happy for me and Megan. Ringing the cancer bell moment was something I had imagined myself doing for a long time, ever since I noticed other people ringing cancer bells to signify the end of their own respective treatments on social media.

Since I had two cancers on my right side: right neck lymph nodes and above my right shoulder blade, my powerport device Is on my left side below my shoulder and above my left breast. I can no longer have a shoulder bag because it aggravates my cancer.

I am not able to carry a purse either because I have neuropathy in both my hands. So, a fanny pack is my go-to like a purse for the last five years and until I die, I suppose!

CHAPTER 24: REGULAR CHECK-UPS ARE A MUST

I am still being checked for my ovarian cancer level, blood tests, mammogram, etc. and follow up with Dr. Hantel, MD and I will be for the rest of my life. In addition to my regular annual physical check-up, etc. I am glad that I am being monitored healthwise, though. That is the only way to find out if I have another cancer and if I do, then I will be treated again.

It is also important to note that Edward-Elmhurst Hospital has helped me out financially with my hospital and doctors expenses for a few years. Whatever my Medicare A and B insurance did not cover, the hospital covered. That was a huge help for me financially. I don't have to worry about my medical expenses and just focus on being better and healthier.

Although I haven't asked for their help the last couple of years, I appreciate everything! Thank you very much. Please continue on helping others as well. May GOD continue on blessing everyone at that hospital and especially the cancer center doctors, nurses, staff and Edward-Elmhurst Hospital itself.

Because of the side effects of chemotherapy treatments, I

stopped taking the Back on Track workouts for cancer patients. I developed neuropathy in both my hands and feet, I can no longer walk miles per week and I could not do any lifting at all. Add to that, the pain in my right arm caused by lymphedema. This was the program that I truly enjoyed participating in since I met so many friends there. I was really disappointed but I had no other choice. I made some new friends with the cancer patients, our trainers and staff at the Edward-Elmhurst Hospital Health Center. They were a bunch of nice and kind people. I surely miss all of them. I hope that they are all doing well in life!

Because of my ongoing cancer that keeps coming back and the side effects of chemotherapy and other treatments, as I said before, I was declared as disabled in 2015. It was like a forced retirement on my part as I couldn't work anymore. I could not concentrate on anything and I have the chemotherapy side effects to blame. I was not ready to retire yet but I really did not have any other choice. The sad part was saying goodbye to my accounting clients. They all understood and wished me the best of luck.

CHAPTER 25: REMISSION RENOVATION

After dealing with so many cancers in the last few years, I neglected to keep my house in tip-top shape. Most of my time, if not all, was consumed with cancer, surgeries, treatments and side effects. I didn't have the time or the energy for anything else. The roof shingles were flying off the roof everytime we had strong winds. Then, we had a stronger wind and hail storm one night and a lot of the shingles came off the roof. They landed in my yard and some in my neighbor's yards. It was really embarrassing, but I just did not have the energy and the mental ability to do anything else. The side effects of chemotherapy and the cancer were debilitating. After my last chemo in June 2016, I finally had the energy to call a roofer and had the roof replaced in September 2016.

Our front yard fence had also started to fall apart. Since Megan and I are pretty handy people, we bought some lumber, screws, bags of cement and replaced the rotting front yard split-rail fence ourselves. We did it after the roof was replaced.

Megan also decided to replace the kitchen flooring herself. It was a challenging and fun thing to do for her. It also saved us some money by doing it herself. She did an excellent job! Thanks, Megan! Slowly but surely, we are catching up with a lot of things that we needed to get done for the house. There were so many things to do. It was mentally, emotionally, physically and financially exhausting to think about and see all the things we needed to do, fix and or replace. I can not believe that the work easily piled up in 6 years time.

Our neighbors and friends, father and son, Steve and Connor helped us maintain the lawn in the summertime and shoveled the driveway in the wintertime. Before Steve and Connor, other neighbors named Kayla and her brother Joe helped us mow the lawn and shovel the driveway. Brothers Pat and Wally helped us with replacing the faucets inside and outside the house, cleaned the gutter, worked on the cars, and replaced the water heater. Now, it is another neighbor named Sami who is helping us mow the front lawn. And I mow the back lawn. To this day, I can always rely on them except for Kayla, Joe, and Connor who moved out of state. Thank you, guys. Megan and I are very appreciative.

CHAPTER 26: A GREAT GARDEN APPEARS

Goodbye to our 34-Year-Old Weeping Willow Tree

In July 2017, our 34 year old beautiful and majestic willow tree dropped a huge branch, broke off, split into two and part of it landed on my neighbor's backyard split rail fence. According to the tree cutter, the inside of the tree was dying and the tree would die sooner than later. To prevent more damage to our property and neighbor's property, Megan and I decided to have the willow tree cut down. It cost Megan almost $3,000.00 to have the fallen branch removed, tree cut down and the stump grinded. 7 hours later, our beautiful and huge weeping willow tree was gone.

There was a big crane truck that the tree workers parked in my backyard and it took 4 guys to cut down and mulch the tree in 7 hours. Megan and I loved that tree so much. It was always one of our most favorite things about where we live. It gave us privacy for many years. Megan and her friends used to swing on it when they were kids. Needless to say, it was a really hard decision to cut it down and it was even harder to watch it be cut down. However, we couldn't risk dropping more branches and doing more damage to our property and others.

Now that the willow tree was gone, we had no other option but to build a backyard fence for privacy. Since our backyard backs to a pond, people are walking around the pond and now with the tree gone, we had no privacy from our neighbors or the pond-goers. Someone had tried to break into our house a few years prior too through our back door. According to the police, the perpetrators tried to break into 3 houses through the back doors, including ours, and all 3 houses did not have a fenced yard.

So, we went fencing. Now, our entire backyard is fenced in instead of being open with a giant willow tree. It was a big change for sure and we still miss the tree, but it is nice having the security of a private fenced in yard.

Now that our backyard was basically a blank canvas, Megan decided to convert our backyard into an amazing flower and vegetable garden. We even built our own raised bed veggie garden! I have never seen so many varieties of flowers, herbs, and vegetables in my whole life. We now have so many flowers, including hydrangeas, dahlias, tulips, crocuses, 18 varieties of roses, etc. The veggies are tomatoes, cucumbers, sweet peppers, green beans, pea pods, etc. Herbs such as oregano, parsley, rosemary, etc. Fruits like strawberries, grapes, raspberries, blackberries, and blueberries.

She also planted garlic, something we both excitedly wait to harvest every year! She plants them sometime in November and she harvests them in July of the following year. So it takes about eight months before the harvesting happens. But it surely is worth the wait! Fresh garlic from the garden is sweet and crunchy. You can literally eat them raw. There's really no comparison from the garlic we buy at the grocery store.

She obviously has a green thumb that she got from her dad and grandpa. It has been 4 years now since she started with her garden and she is still very much involved in planting different things every year. She's grown two pumpkins that she made fresh pumpkin pies for Thanksgiving dessert last year. She just harvested the pumpkin that she grew this year and will be ready for pie baking next month's Thanksgiving dinner dessert. She takes really good care of her plants by watering, fertilizing, and harvesting them herself. Those flowers and vegetables thrive every single year. I have never eaten so many fresh vegetables and fruits until the last 4 years. It is such a treat and nothing compares to a homegrown tomato! Thanks so much, Meg!

Gardening serves as Megan's outlet for what we both went through with my ovarian cancer, surgeries, chemotherapy, and the side effects for six years. It allows her to make sense of the chaos. She finds the whole plant process to be very rewarding and fulfilling.

We also enjoy fresh flowers all year round too because Megan plants indoor flowers as well like paperwhites, amaryllis, etc. for the winter season. May GOD continue on blessing you with excellent health and everything, Meg! Love you!

CHAPTER 27: THE DAY THE FENCE ALMOST TOOK US OUT

In September 2017, both Megan and I were in the backyard doing some yard work. I was on the outside of the fence, while she was on the inside of the fence. It was a very windy day and a super strong gust came through that ended up ripping the fence gate off its hardware and dropping it outside our new fence. I ran towards Megan because I was not so sure what that loud noise was and if she was okay. She, after witnessing the whole incident ran towards me to make sure I was okay.

After the shock wore off, we both picked up the gate and tried to screw it back on the posts but, since one of the posts was already damaged, we could not put it back on. I went to the hardware store and bought the things I needed to fix the gate. Thankfully, we were able to fix it. That was a very scary moment!

Then that same night, I felt pain in my right wrist. I must have twisted my wrist while lifting the heavy fence gate. I just took some Extra Strength Tylenol thinking that the pain will go away. It did but just for a short time. I wore wrist support to prevent me from using my right hand.

Actually the wrist support was Megan's when she sprained her left wrist years ago. This was my right wrist. I just tried to use what we already have. Hoping that my right wrist will be pain free eventually and I will be able to use my right hand again. I am right handed so it was a challenge for me to function normally. I later found out that wearing the left wrist support to help my right wrist literally slowed the healing process. Now, I must admit that it was a really dumb idea! I could have just gone to the store and bought the wrist support for my right wrist but I didn't.

CHAPTER 28: COMPRESSION SLEEVES AND PHYSICAL THERAPY

I needed to have compression sleeves fitted for my right arm because of my lymphedema. I was having constant pain during that time. I called and made an appointment at Edward-Elmhurst Hospital's Physical Therapy Department which is located in another location but still in Naperville.

So, off I went for my appointment. It was then that the physical therapist supervisor noticed the wrist support I was wearing on my right wrist. She asked me what happened and I told her about the fence gate that was lifted by the strong winds and my daughter and I lifted the gate back where it belonged. I said I must have lifted it the wrong way because it has been hurting since then. She asked me if I have seen a physical therapist. I told her that I hadn't. She told me that she would call in one of the physical therapists there that could help me. Then, she also said, "by the way, the wrist support you are wearing is supposedly for the left wrist." I smiled and I said that I knew that and it was my daughter's when she sprained her left wrist years ago. I was just trying to use what I already had.

My right arm was measured for the compression sleeve. Also, the physical therapy for my right wrist started that same night. I learned a lot from that physical therapy. I can not remember how many sessions I went in for but it surely helped my wrist in getting back to normal. One thing I noticed after my chemotherapy is my bones are not normal anymore. They are weak and somewhat brittle now.

To this day, aside from having neuropathy in both my hands and feet, both my wrists and ankles are sensitive. One of the reasons why I wear compression gloves at night and sometimes during the day as well.

I can vividly remember my racquetball days. I would climb the side of the racquetball court just so I do not miss a shot. It did not matter to me who I was playing against whether it was a male or a female or he or she was my boss.

I always wanted to play my best and win. For the majority of the games I played, I did win! I have always been very competitive in sports and in everything I do. But, I can not do any of those things anymore. Maybe, it's partly because of my age (68 years old) and the majority of it is from the side effects of chemotherapy. I just blame everything on chemotherapy nowadays. Haha!

CHAPTER 29: HOME RENOVATION CONTINUES

I t was also in 2017 when we had all our windows that were very hard and loud to open and one sliding door replaced for efficiency. Our 2nd-floor deck and railings were replaced as well by professionals. By this time Megan and I had done a number of DIY projects as home improvements ourselves for the most part. But, there are still a lot of things to do. These things are not needed to be done for luxury but for necessity.

We had problems with the contractor who replaced the 2nd-floor deck and railing and supposedly fixed the water leak from the deck to the 1st-floor living room. The water leak was not fixed. The rainwater was still leaking into our 1st-floor living room from the 2nd-floor deck. So, I called him a few times to come back and fix it.

I must have called him about 4 times. The 4th time I reminded him about the roofer who replaced my roof the year prior. I told this contractor what Doug, the roofer, promised me. The roofer said, **"I will do a good job the first time, so I don't have to come back the second time to fix my mistake"**. He was a man of his words and I have not called him back because he did a good job the first time. Now, this contractor had been back 4 times and he was not happy every time I called him to come back and fix the problem. I was not happy either having him in my house that many times.

He even loudly jumped on the 2nd-floor deck while I was in the 1st-floor living room, to intimidate me, but I was not intimidated. I told him that if he still can not fix this problem today, I do not want him to come back to my house anymore. I will call another handyman to fix the problem. I guess he was not expecting me to say that to him because he looked very surprised. He finally was able to fix the leak the 4th time that he was here. I am not sure what he did differently but he was able to fix it.

So, it is safe to say that I will never recommend him to others. My mistake was I gave him an outstanding online review because he politely asked me right after he was done replacing the deck and railings.

Then this happened. From that time on when a contractor asks me for a 5-star review online, I make sure that the work is done to my satisfaction first and wait a few days before the review. Lesson learned!

CHAPTER 30: MY SISTER TESS DIED UNEXPECTEDLY

My sister Tess died unexpectedly on June 21, 2018, of a heart attack and stroke at the young age of 67 years old. Since this is probably the only book that I will write in my lifetime, I would like to honor my sister Tess by including her story here. Yesterday was her birthday, October 3rd. She would have been 70 years old.

The years 2017 to 2021 were good years for me. I did not have any new cancer, no new surgeries, no chemotherapy treatments, and not dealing with any side effects.

So, I was finally getting back to my normal life. Then on June 21, 2018, my sister Tess died unexpectedly.

She had gone on a long weekend trip with her friends and on the day that she was to return home she fainted, and had a heart attack and stroke. She suffered for 10 excruciating painful days in a hospital, far away from her home before going back home in ashes. She left behind her husband, Lito of many years, two sons, Paolo and Rael, in-laws Jhen, Angel, and grandchildren Gabby, Blue, and Kahel.

Tess was three years older than me and she was the oldest of six children. I looked up to her as my mentor. When we were growing up, I used to do everything she did and followed her wherever she went. Come to think of it now, I was the pain in her behind.

I know I mentioned her name a few times in this book. Every time I think of her it reminds me of what I posted on social media a couple of years ago. "You know you are healed and done grieving when you can tell your story without crying". I guess I am not done grieving and not healed yet because I still get emotional when I think and talk about her. Tears rolled down my face while I was writing this.

Tess was the kind of person who thought of others first before herself. She was a caring, loving, kind, and generous human being who helped a lot of people in her lifetime. There were hundreds of people who showed up during her wake to pay their final respects and said their goodbyes. Sadly, I was not able to go to her wake.

According to my younger sister Lynne, there was this lady who told her that our sister Tess was giving her money for food every month since she had a car accident and lost her job.

Nobody knew that my sister Tess was doing that for a stranger. Not even her husband, Lito. Tess heard about that lady's story and my sister Tess reached out to her and started helping her out financially.

There were many more stories from her friends that we did not know about. Tess was the kind of person who would help others without expecting anything in return. She extended help to others quietly. She did not need the acknowledgment and fanfare. She just helped people because it was the right thing to do. **My niece Shelly was the one who delivered Tess' eulogy. "Shelly said that her auntie Tess was not a movie star, not a politician, not a famous person but she touched a lot of people's lives in her lifetime because she was a kind, generous, caring, and loving human being"!** I can just imagine how emotional people were when Shelly was saying those words. My younger sister Lynne has now taken on our sister Tess' legacy by helping others. Thanks, sister Lynne. Keep up the kind and good work! By the way, the word "sistoy" means sister. My sister Tess and I came up with that word years ago for affection.

You may recall during my chemotherapy treatments the significance of a cardinal bird to me. That a loved one is visiting you when you see a cardinal bird. Well, after my sister Tess died, I have seen so many cardinals in my front yard, and backyard, and when I checked the mail once, a cardinal flew to the side of my head. Tess was probably telling me to stop crying because she's happy where she is now.

I still see cardinals to this day but not as frequently as when Tess just died. I pray and talk to my sister Tess and my mom every time I see a cardinal bird.

Megan and I created a special spot for Tess in our garden. Megan plants white flowers every year for Tess because white was her favorite color. Also, Megan and I created a spot next to Tess for my mom. Megan plants pink flowers for my mom every year.

When she was still alive we used to call each other and say we love each other before we hung up the phone. I find comfort in knowing that we were able to say we love each other before that fatal long weekend trip with her friends. I wish that she was still alive and healthy because there are so many things I wanted to tell her. I miss and love you so much, sistoy! Until we all see each other, mom, dad, and now brother Rico too. Love you all so much. Rest easy!

CHAPTER 31: PAINTING THROUGH GRIEF

Since I was having a difficult time accepting that my sister Tess is already gone, I thought of painting the inside of my house to keep myself busy. Boy did I keep busy! Our house really needed it too given that most of our walls still had the original wallpaper and paint. I started by painting just the doors from their old and boring dark brown color to all white. I did not realize that there are 17 doors in this small house including the closet doors. Once I did that, we realized that the dark brown baseboards needed to be painted white to match the doors as well. Painting all the baseboards in the house was a project within itself. What a difference it made though!

It was all worth the physical pain I experienced with my hands and feet neuropathy. We went from having a very dark and drabby 80s house to a fresh and bright modern house.

Then I painted the walls and ceilings of my bedroom, the living room, the two bathrooms, the closets, the kitchen, the kitchen cabinets, the bathroom cabinets, the moldings, shutters, and trim. Megan painted her bedroom and closet. I painted my bedroom pink for the breast cancer color to remind me every day of how thankful and grateful I am that I am still around.

White was my color of choice in painting most of it except for the bedrooms, bathrooms, and the accent hallway that I painted green. By painting the inside of the house white, it looks a lot bigger than it actually is and cleaner.

Because I have neuropathy in both my hands and feet due to the side effects of chemotherapy treatments and lymphedema on my right arm and armpit, I worked maybe three times slower than normal people would. I was in a lot of pain most of the time too, therefore more Extra Strength Tylenol was needed. Actually, It took me over 6 months to finish painting the inside of the house. I also installed elbow brackets on shelves that were warping, installed kitchen cabinet handles, etc. It kept me busy and there was something for me to look forward to every day. It helped me not to think of my sister Tess a lot.

I can honestly tell you though that I do not want to see a single can of paint for as long as I live!

Keep on Keeping on, Home Projects

Megan and I are still catching up with all the things we needed to do for the home that we put on hold for years while I was dealing with cancer. Little by little and one day at a time, we are making progress but it is costing us a lot of money. Thank goodness that we are both handy and did most of these things ourselves except for the ones that we are just not capable of doing. I replaced the bathroom floor. Megan and I replaced all of the window treatments. Then the water heater stopped working, so off to Home Depot. Thankfully, we had our friend Pat replace it again. The water heater was replaced 3 years ago and here we are replacing it again.

Then, the garage door needed to be replaced since the wood was starting to rot. I called several garage door companies and we found one in town that was having a sale on garage doors and installation for senior citizens. Very reasonable price. I thought he was going to be here all day long but it only took him a few hours to remove the old garage door and replace it with a new white garage door. He did a good job in such a short time. He said the old garage door will be recycled, which I was happy to hear.

Our driveway had not been seal coated in years, so it was finally done. We got a great discount from the company too from the incredibly nice husband and wife team (Paula and Javier) that owns the P&J Sealcoating Company. They have been helping us every year since then.

Three of the sidewalk square concrete were also sinking. It just happened that the township lowered their rate per square that year so we had them replaced. Also, we needed them replaced to avoid potential accidents of people walking on the sidewalk. I tell you when it rains it really pours!

CHAPTER 32: 2020 COVID-19 PANDEMIC

2020 is the year that nobody will ever forget when the Covid-19 pandemic took over the whole world. That was a very tense and scary year. We did not know anything about that virus. Many senior citizens and vulnerable people died and are still dying. Lockdowns, social distancing, washing hands frequently. No social gatherings. We, like so many others, were not able to see our friends and family. Megan bought a pair of hair scissors and she was able to cut my hair and her own hair as well.

In February 2020 before the pandemic really hit here, Megan and I went shopping for a new living room floor. This was a project that we had wanted to do for a long time, but other, more necessary projects kept getting in the way.

We bought the planks and other materials we needed. By this time, because of all our bad experiences with contractors, they are no longer welcome, needed, or wanted in our house anymore. We will do everything that we possibly can ourselves and this was a project that we knew we could do.

We removed the old carpet, washed the concrete floor, and applied a solution to clean the floor, and for the new plank tiles to stick. The process is a hard and time-consuming job but we saved a lot of money by doing it ourselves. Also, it saved us from headaches dealing with contractors. Then after a day when the concrete floor was all dried up, Megan replaced the living room floor and hallway all by herself for 19 hours straight. She did not stop until it was completely finished. She only took 2 breaks to eat lunch and dinner. I could not help her anymore as my whole body was in pain and falling apart. Megan, as always, did an excellent job. It looked like it was done by a professional! I am always so proud of her!

Just a couple of weeks later and March 2020 started with lockdowns, social distancing, and washing hands frequently. This was the month and year that we started ordering groceries and dinner online with no contact delivery from March 2020 to May 2021 and delivered in front of our garage door.

Then we take the groceries and food inside the garage, leave them in the garage for about 15 minutes, and disinfect every single item in the kitchen sink before putting them away.

It took us one hour to disinfect every single grocery item. We did this process for 14 months. Also, when we order restaurant delivery, we heat them up in the oven first before eating them every single time.

We did all of these precautionary measures because of me. I belong to the high-risk group. It cost us more money with tips and everything but it was better safe than sorry! Like everyone else, we did not get to see our friends and family for a long time. Except for my best friend, Beth and her daughter Kendall who dropped off delicious dinner many times. They left them in my front door without coming inside the house to protect me. We only saw them through the glass storm door. That's how kind and thoughtful they are!

April 2020. I got a call from nurse Maria, my oncologist's Dr. Hantel's nurse and she canceled my regular ovarian cancer level, blood tests, and follow-up with Dr. Hantel. Because I was included in the high-risk group, she said for me to stay far away from the hospital. By this time Megan and I were more careful than ever.

CHAPTER 33: MY 17-YEAR-OLD NIECE KENDALL

I t was still April 2020 when I found out that my niece Kendall started her own baking business at the very young age of 17 years old. She was a junior in high school. She is a very smart, talented, and caring person, just like her mom Beth who is my ultimate best friend. Kendall donated dozens of high-end cupcakes to the first responders, and the fire and police departments in her hometown of Roselle, IL in order to thank them for what they do.

Since I have been going to Edward-Elmhurst Hospital and the Cancer Center for many years, I asked Kendall if she would make cupcakes for the nurses, doctors, and medical staff of the hospital and cancer center, to show appreciation for risking their own lives to help others during the pandemic.

She happily said yes and that she would love to help. She donated and delivered 6 dozen high-end cupcakes to the cancer center and hospital while celebrating her mom's birthday that day. Everyone appreciated it and was grateful for the delicious cupcakes. They later found out that Kendall was only 17 years old. They were more impressed by her kindness, talent, and creativity! I do not remember what I was doing when I was 17 years old but, I definitely was not helping other people the way that she was. She also donated a few dozen cupcakes to the Lisle Fire Department which was very much appreciated by everyone.

Because she thought and helped others first, her selfless act of donating cupcakes to the frontliners and first responders, she was featured in a local newspaper and magazine. In one of those interviews, Kendall said, **"Everyone is always so brightened because I think baked goods really hit people's hearts" and "I love making people's day. I just love giving to people."** Those nice articles about her are on their websites as well. Patch.com and GlancerMagazine.com. However, her baking business is on hold for now as she attends college on a full academic scholarship. I can already tell how bright her future will be! Keep up the good work, Smenge! Words are not enough to express how proud I am of her. Thanks so much, Kendall! I appreciate you more than you will ever know. Love ya and GOD bless always!!!

CHAPTER 34:
EXPENSES WE
DID NOT EXPECT
BUT NEEDED

I think it was May 2020, still during the height of the pandemic when the TV in our living room stopped working. This was the time when we were not allowed to go outside because of covid-19. Watching TV was one of those things we did to pass time.

This was really bad timing for the TV to die. I couldn't bear the thought of missing my daily and weekly shows. Haha. It would have driven both of us crazy without the TV. So, Megan measured the size of the TV that would fit in the entertainment center. She got online and started looking for some sales on TV and free delivery.

She found and bought one and the new TV was delivered the following day. No contact delivery, of course! We asked the delivery guys to just leave the TV still in a big box outside our garage door. As soon as those two delivery guys left, Megan and I carried the TV inside the house. Opened the box, put the TV together, and placed it in the same entertainment center where the old TV was. And, just like that, the problem was solved!

Here, I was thinking how are we going to get rid of the old 64" TV? Well, I remember that there are a couple of guys driving pickup trucks around the neighborhood twice a week and picking up anything metal. But this is not metal. I thought, what have we got to lose? If they don't pick it up, then we will just drive it to and drop it off at the recycling center for a small fee. So, Megan and I carried and placed the old TV and taped the remote control on top of the TV in our driveway. Surprisingly, the TV was picked up in only about 15 minutes. I was looking out the kitchen window when a guy in a pickup truck came. I think it was a coincidence that the guy in a pickup truck was driving around the neighborhood when we just happened to put out the TV in our driveway. Lucky for us! I can not believe that the old TV was gone in such a short time but it was! Goodbye old and not working anymore TV and welcome lifesaver new TV!!

Central Air Goes Kaput During a Heat Wave

One hot summer day, we realized that the air had stopped working. At this point, I asked myself what else could go wrong. Then, I thought it was still 2020! So, that answered my question. We called a few A/C and heating companies. Two people came from two different companies to give us an estimate on how much it would cost to fix or replace the entire unit. It was a 15-year-old unit and they both said it will be cheaper to replace it than to fix it.

So, replacing the A/C unit was our only option. Since the company that we chose was all booked up for the next two weeks, we waited for two long extremely hot weeks until it was replaced. Another expense that we were not expecting and it was expensive! But, it is material and not a health problem. So, we are good! Again, like I said a few times before, we all need to appreciate anything and everything in life and this was one of those things.

CHAPTER 35: PANDEMIC FIRST CANCER CHECK-UPS

This was now in June 2020 my first appointment for 2020 since my April 2020 appointment was canceled because of the covid-19 pandemic. To tell you the truth I felt like canceling this appointment myself. I did not know what to expect to show up at the cancer center because there is still a lot that we do not know about the virus during this time. I was afraid that I might catch covid at the hospital. But I was really surprised to see how organized the hospital and the cancer center were.

When I entered the door of the cancer center, there were people who were giving the patients masks, taking our temperature (if your temperature is high they will not let us in), we were given hand sanitizer, 6 feet social distance, and I was shown the room where the nurse was for my cancer level and blood tests.

Remember, I have a powerport device implant so not all nurses are certified to access powerport devices but this nurse was. Thankfully, she was able to access my power port easily with no problem. Before this, she took my temperature again, my blood pressure, and my weight. Then I was sent upstairs on the 2nd floor to wait for my oncologist, Dr. Hantel.

My oncologist came into the room and we talked a little bit about the pandemic. He was proud to tell me that no one in the hospital has been infected by covid-19 except for a patient who lied about not traveling outside the country and the doctor who treated that patient but they both recovered.

I was happy to know that such a big hospital was so prepared and so organized that no other employees have been infected. Then, he told me about the results of my blood tests. The blood test results were all good! I had to wait for my ovarian cancer level test results which normally come out later than the blood test results. I got the results as soon as I got home and my ovarian cancer level result is one of the lowest again. Thank GOD!

Mammogram, Ultrasound, Breast Needle Biopsy Left Breast

It was still the covid-19 year 2020 and I needed to go back to the hospital in order to stay on schedule with my breast cancer monitoring.

It was September 24, 2020, during my 6-month regular mammogram when a nodule in my left breast was found. I said to myself, "here we go again". An ultrasound and a breast needle biopsy were done, too. The breast ultrasound was a breeze but the needle biopsy was not. It was painful. I should really be used to the needle biopsy by now since I already have a few during my cancer journey but, I am not and it is still painful as heck. I hope that one of these days, someone will be able to invent the mammogram machine that will not hurt so much. After the above procedures were done, as always, I patiently and anxiously waited for the results.

Then the doctor/radiologist with the mammography technician

came out of the room and told me that the result was benign, not malignant! No new cancer! That was great news! They also said that I needed to come back in six months for a follow-up mammogram. Thank GOD, it is not another cancer!

I was so happy and at the same time could not wait until I got out of the hospital because I was afraid that I would catch covid-19 while there from other patients.

Although Edward-Elmhurst Hospital did a great job on their precautionary measures on the covid-19 and extremely clean hospital, I was still not comfortable with all the patients coming in and out of the hospital. Because you don't know who those people are and where they came from.

As soon as I got home, I washed the clothes I was wearing and I took a shower. You probably remember by now that every time I go to the hospital, I would go straight to the bathroom and shower at home. Although Edward-Elmhurst Hospital is probably the cleanest hospital I have been to, you can probably eat off the floor. I just don't like the smell of the hospital. The hospital smells like medicine to me. I feel sick when I smell medicine. Haha!

More Ovarian Cancer, Blood Tests, and Check-Ups

Since it was still a covid-19 pandemic year, I already knew the drill at this time. Wear a mask, social distance, and use a hand sanitizer. A hospital employee was at the entrance of the building taking people's temperatures before I was told to check in with the receptionist on the 2nd floor. I waited in the waiting room and the nurse called me to take my weight, blood pressure, and temperature again before she accessed my powerport for my ovarian cancer level and blood tests and flush my power port before and after with saline and heparin. The nurse was good. She was able to access my powerport with no problems.

Then I waited for Dr. Hantel, my oncologist. He checked my breathing, my neck where one of the cancers was, my back, and my breasts. You may recall that I had breast cancer in both my breasts. Then he told me that my blood test results were normal. Also, my ovarian cancer level is good. Thank GOD again and again!

When I returned for another check-up in January 2021 at the cancer center building, I was surprised that there was no employee waiting to check our temperature before entering the building. The receptionist told me that as long as we are wearing masks and socially distanced they don't need to check our temperature anymore. Woah! That was a very good sign that things are improving! So happy to hear that!

So, I went upstairs on the 2nd floor like I normally would for my ovarian cancer level and blood tests. This time I do not need to see Dr. Hantel for a follow-up. This would be the first time that I only need to see him every six months now unless my cancer comes back. The results will be on mychart and Dr. Hantel will read the results and will make a comment for me to read. The results are all good. My cancer level is one of the lowest and my blood test results are normal. Another great and encouraging news! I pray and hope that more great news is coming for many more years to come. I am truly Blessed and lucky. Thank you, GOD!

CHAPTER 36:
BLURRY VISION AND
NEW GLASSES

My eyesight was getting blurry so I made an appointment to have my eyes checked. I was afraid that I might have cancer in my eyes. I was actually worried that precautions might not be taken at this office. But, I was totally wrong. They are taking every precaution that I could think of. The office was by appointment only and no other people/patients are allowed in the office at all.

Once I was in the parking lot and still in my car, I called them and that was when they asked me questions including insurance information before they say you can go to the door but wear a mask. Then someone opened the door wearing a mask and took my temperature first before escorting me to the room for the initial eye tests.

Then, Dr. Garvey, the optometrist, came and took me to another room for a more thorough examination. The result of the examination was good and I thankfully did not have cancer in my eyes. My eyes prescription did not change a lot. After the exam, I was taken back to the front office which has plexiglass between Audrey the office manager, and me to choose the glasses frame that I wanted. She explained the price difference between the frames that I chose. I chose the best for my budget after my insurance's share of the cost. I am very impressed that they do all these safety and precautionary steps.

I had to make another appointment in order to pick up my new glasses. Again, I called from the parking lot. I was still in my car. I waited until one of their patients was out of the office before they let me in. I had my mask on and so did Audrey. I tried on the prescription glasses. They were good. Then she gave me a nice glasses holder and I left. It only took me around 10 minutes. Since Dr. Garvey gave me my new prescription reading glasses grade. I was able to buy more reading glasses online because I have been forgetting and losing my reading glasses everywhere I go. I bought a total of 18 extra pairs of reading glasses online to be exact. Now I have more glasses than I need and I can afford to lose a pair or two or more. I gave away 2 pairs to my cousins. I already lost 2 pairs as of this writing. Apparently, when you have so many glasses they can be easier to lose!

CHAPTER 37: MAMMOGRAM AND MORE CHECK-UPS

I t has been six months since my last mammogram. So, here we go again with my follow-up mammogram. No employee was at the entrance of the hospital taking our temperature before we entered the building. I went directly to the Mammography Department. Although they were not taking our temperature anymore, the seating arrangement is still socially distant, which I really like. Then the painful mammogram started. I think both my breasts are getting so used to the pain, that those mammography machines are responsible for giving to the patients that I now feel numb. After it was over, the technician asked me to wait in the waiting room for the result. So, again I waited nervously, but patiently.

The technician came out of the room smiling and told me that there was no need for an ultrasound and biopsy because there was no change in my mammogram results from six months ago. That was great news! The doctor/radiologist said I do not need to come back for a follow-up in six months but come back in a year instead. That's great! I am starting to be like a normal woman who only goes for a mammogram once a year. Instead of every six months that I have been going.

Wow, I was so happy to hear this, I could not wait to tell Megan and my best bud Beth! I also could not wait until I was out of the hospital for fear that I might catch something that would make me sick. It is still covid-19 year after all. I am so blessed! Thank you, GOD!!! Then as soon as I got home I washed my clothes and took a shower. Maybe my nickname should be the "shower lady". Haha!

I was due for yet another cancer level check-up. Like last January 2021, the cancer center was back to normal. There weren't any employees checking people's temperature by the hospital's entrance, but we still wore masks, used hand sanitizer, and social distance. I proceeded to go upstairs to the 2nd floor to have my ovarian cancer level, blood tests, and follow-up with Dr. Hantel.

As usual, my powerport was accessed and flushed with saline and heparin before and after with no problem by one of the nurses. Then I saw Dr. Hantel. Again, I was checked and he discussed with me the result of my mammogram which was good. No new cancer. My blood test results are normal and my ovarian cancer level is good!

Again after I was sent home from the cancer center, I went straight home instead of going to the grocery store first which was my plan. I took a shower and I took a long nap. It was a long and very good nap. I was mentally and physically exhausted by now. I felt like I had exhausted my energy for the day. It was a well-deserved nap and helped me energize my mind and body.

CHAPTER 38:
COVID-19 PFIZER
VACCINES

I was lucky enough to be able to sign up for the first vaccine pretty easily because of my high-risk status. The hospital had its own system set up for those that belonged to their network and I was able to get the first vaccine a stone's throw away from my house in one of the hospital's fitness buildings.

There were many people in the building but there were a lot of nurses as well. I was surprised and amazed at how organized, efficient and professional the employees were. The line was moving at a very fast pace.

It only took less than 5 minutes to wait and be vaccinated. Then, I was given my COVID-19 vaccine ID card. I had to wait another 15 minutes to relax in case there was a complication with the vaccine. Meanwhile, there were a number of employees going around asking people if they needed help. I flagged one of them to help me set up my next appointment online. She did and then I was out the door.

As soon as I got home I took a shower, washed my clothes, and then rested. I immediately felt the side effects of the vaccine.

My left arm where I had the vaccine was getting heavier. I felt feverish and had a mild headache. I had some soup and crackers. I also drank plenty of water. I took some Extra Strength Tylenol and applied a cold compressor to the affected area. It was a 24-hour side effect and I was fine the following day.

3 weeks later I had my 2nd Pfizer vaccine at the same place where I had the first one. Again, I was amazed at how organized and efficient this process was. The employees were all trained and professional. The whole process only took about 10 minutes. The nurse filled out the second date on my COVID-19 vaccine ID card. The nurse also told me that this COVID-19 vaccine ID card is very important and I should put it in a safe place.

Again as soon as I got home, I took a shower, washed my clothes, took 2 Extra Strength Tylenol, and used a cold compressor on my left arm in that area where I was vaccinated. Had a bowl of soup, crackers, and plenty of water to drink. Then I took a nap. I was having a hard time moving my left arm, but I was fine the following day.

6 months after that I went in for my first booster shot. This was at a different location than the first two covid-19 vaccines. Again, the staff was well prepared. They were all nice and professional from the receptionist and the employee who escorted me to nurse Laurie. There was no wait.

The rain was pouring like crazy that day. It was a little challenging going to a place I have not been to before and getting used to driving a new vehicle. I missed my turn because I could not see the road. It only took about 5 minutes for the whole process.

I was able to go grocery shopping and got a haircut after. I did not feel the side effects until the following day. My left arm got heavier, and I had a fever twice, chills and lightheadedness. I woke up a few times in the middle of the night feeling cold and sweaty. The side effects on me were two days after the shot. After 2 days I was back to normal.

CHAPTER 39: NEW PRIMARY DOCTOR

I had my annual physical examination. I was given cognitive and eye tests, pneumonia shots, etc. Then I got to meet Dr. Straczynski, MD who was recommended to me by my oncologist, Dr. Hantel, MD. I replaced my old primary doctor because she was not part of the Edward-Elmhurst Doctors' network.

Dr. Straczynski, MD suggested that I have a DEXA bone density scan because the last time I had it was years ago. Also, a thyroid scan, blood tests for cholesterol, glucose, etc. Since the cholesterol and glucose are already included on my regular blood tests for my ovarian cancer level tests, she agreed to have it done on my next blood tests but I should fast for 14 hours before the tests.

I am impressed with Dr. Straczynski, MD, and the whole staff at that clinic. They are all so nice, friendly, professional, and knowledgeable.

I am glad that she was referred to me by Dr. Hantel, MD, and she is now my primary doctor. Thank you Dr. Straczynski for being so thorough. Also, her clinic is just 5 minutes away from my home.

DEXA Bone Scan and Thyroid Scan

The Imaging technician was nice and friendly during my bone scan. The whole process took about 15 minutes only. Dr. Straczynski, MD later contacted me with the results. Since I am already taking Vitamin D3 she said to start taking calcium 500mg as well. I have to have my A1C Hemoglobin and lipid panel blood tests again in three months. So, that would be October 2021, and make an appointment to see her again.

The thyroid scan took about 20 minutes only. The technician was nice and a good listener. After the procedure, she said I can go home and the result will take a couple of days and will be forwarded to my doctor. Dr. Straczynski let me know that there are multiple thyroid nodules in my thyroid but they are not cancerous. We will just monitor the multiple nodules and will do another thyroid scan in a year. Thank GOD!!!

My cholesterol is a little elevated and my glucose/blood sugar is borderline diabetes. So I have to redo the same lipid panel/ cholesterol and A1c hemoglobin/glucose/blood sugar tests in three months. And will see Dr. Straczynski then

I did not start monitoring my blood sugar by pricking my fingers until 11/09/2021

I occasionally not every day prick my fingers to get my blood sugar before breakfast and two hours either after lunch or two hours after dinner. The before breakfast number must be below 130. And the two hours after lunch or two hours after dinner must be below 160. So far so good. My numbers are below the threshold almost all the time.

Megan and I try to always have a balanced meal. The list below is food that we consume most of the time:

Breakfast: bananas, fried eggs, ham, white or wheat bread, English muffins, strawberry jam, butter, water, or coffee once in a while

Lunch: sandwiches (ham, eggs, pastrami, corned beef). Salad: romaine lettuce, spinach. Dressings: blue cheese, Caesar, parmesan cheese.

Fruits: blueberries, strawberries, raspberries, mangoes, pineapple, watermelon, cantaloupe, bananas. Nuts: pistachios, peanuts, cashews, almonds

Snacks: nuts, pastry, chips, water

Dinner: meat/protein (pork, beef, fish/salmon, shrimp, eggs), carbs (rice, potatoes, pasta, bread, corn), vegetables (kale, spinach, colored peppers, tomatoes, mushrooms, etc), desserts (ice cream, pies, pastries, cake, cookies)

CHAPTER 40: TRAUMATIC POWERPORT DEVICE EXPERIENCE

It seemed like the cancer center and the hospital was now back to normal. We still wore masks, social distance, and sanitized our hands but no more employees took our temperature at the entrance of the building. So, I went upstairs to the second floor like I normally would. I got in line to let the receptionist know I was already there. Then, I sat and waited for my name to be called. When my name was called and I specifically told the new nurse that I was fasting. The last time I ate was around 10:00 pm the night before.

My appointment was at 1:00 pm. So, that was 15 hours ago. By that time I was already starving. I usually do not fast for my ovarian cancer and blood tests but my new primary doctor, Dr. Straczynski wants accurate results on my A1C hemoglobin glucose and lipid panel/cholesterol. So, I fasted.

It was a new nurse at the cancer center who was assigned to me that day and I will not mention their name in order to protect their identity. That nurse tried so many times to access my powerport and failed.

At some point, they were able to access my powerport but were not able to get blood. I could tell that they were getting frustrated. My patience was running thin at that time as well. They kept trying and trying until I asked them to stop and asked for help from the other nurses. They did but they still could not get blood from my powerport.

So, I requested their supervisor, Derrick, to help me. The nurse supervisor, Derrick, just used my vein and not my powerport. He inserted the needle in my vein in just one try and he got the blood flowing. That was a very painful and traumatic experience for me with that new nurse.

I am sure that it wasn't a great experience for the nurse as well. They kept on saying it was not their fault and things like that happen all the time without apologizing to me. Quite frankly, I don't need an apology. I just don't want another patient to go through what I went through.

I talked with the new nurse before I left and I told them that it was not their fault but they also have to know that I have been coming to the cancer center for the last eleven years total. The first year at the radiation department and ten years here at the chemotherapy department. This has never ever happened to me before. Plus, my powerport was unclogged just 3 months prior.

I said that maybe, next time hopefully, there will not be the next time but, it is okay for you to ask for help from other nurses. Instead of leaving your patients in pain and uncomfortable. I think they understood what I said. I was not planning on telling Dr. Hantel, MD, and nurse Maria of what happened, but as soon as I got home I got a notification from the hospital that my test results were in.

I went online and I got the results of my ovarian cancer level and blood tests. I was reading the results and it says that I did not fast. This was completely wrong because I specifically told that new nurse that I did and it has been 15 hours ago that I ate last. It was 10:00 pm to be exact. Obviously, that new nurse was not paying attention. I also wanted my new primary doctor, Dr. Edyta Straczynski to know that I followed her advice to fast the night before.

So, I called nurse Maria and told her what happened and asked her to say that I fasted on the report. Thank you, nurse Maria. Since I had that traumatic experience with the new nurse, I certainly do not want to go through that again. So every time I go to the cancer center for my ovarian cancer level and blood tests, I always request for another nurse.

I prefer another nurse to avoid having to go through that same traumatic experience with that new nurse again. I will never ever forget the physical pain that that new nurse caused me.

CHAPTER 41: TEETH AND CHEMO, WHO KNEW?

Since I did not go to the dentist at all in 2020 because I was afraid to catch the covid-19 virus from the dentist's office, I needed to have my upper back two teeth checked. Also, one of my friend's daughters got covid-19 from the dentist's office which only made me fear going even more. But, my teeth really started to bother me, so I had to pay my dentist, Dr. Gibson, a visit.

Well, after a complete x-ray and teeth scan, I had two teeth that needed to be extracted or have a root canal. Dr. Gibson is a cosmetic dentist so she does not do either, so I had to look for a dentist that's part of my insurance network.

After calling so many dentists in my area, I found out that they are all doing teeth extraction only and not root canals.

Finally, I found one actually in the same building and same floor as Dr. Gibson's office. Dr. Gibson has been my dentist and friend for well over ten years now. She and her staff (Suzy, former employee, Daisy, Tala) and others are all nice and professional. I always recommend them to friends and family.

This new dentist's name was Dr. John Chae, an oral surgeon and I made an appointment with him. My consultation appointment with him is not until August 26, 2021. I had almost a month to wait. It was a good thing that I was not in pain. I just used the left side of my teeth to chew on food. But, I was also putting too much pressure on my left teeth because normally I use both sides to chew on food. I hoped that I didn't cause any problems with my left teeth too. This is all part of my chemotherapy side effects. My teeth are now weak. I did not have this problem before.

My appointment finally came and I was able to see the new dentist. They took another x-ray of my whole mouth in addition to the x-ray of my individual teeth Dr. Gibson's office sent him. Dr. John looked very young and was a nice dentist. He explained to me the pros and cons of tooth extraction. I said I know and I already made my decision.

Since both teeth are next to each other and they are on the upper back part of my mouth, and I am the only one who can see them, I want both teeth extracted so I don't have to worry about tooth decay and gum disease.

He was able to extract both teeth within 15 minutes. He was a good oral surgeon. I did not feel any pain. I said I will just take Extra Strength Tylenol as soon as I get home. He wrote a pain killer prescription and antibiotics. But, I did not buy them. I got what I needed at home antibiotics and Extra Strength Tylenol. I started taking them as soon as I got home from his office.

He called me that night and was just checking up on me. I thought that it was very nice of him to call and follow up with his patients after office hours. I said that I was fine, I was just a little sore. He said that I would be sore for a few days. He used soluble stitches, so I do not need to come back to the office. The stitches will dissolve in a week or two.

I said that this is just one of those challenges that I have to overcome. With what I went through with 6 cancers, surgeries, treatments, and side effects, this is nothing! He said, "wow, I had no idea you went through so much already". He also said that he was inspired by my story.

CHAPTER 42: OFFICIALLY DECLARED IN REMISSION

But, Another Ovarian Cancer Level And Blood Tests Check-Up First. Well, time for my regular ovarian cancer level test, blood tests, and a follow-up appointment with my oncologist, Dr. Hantel. The cancer center was again busy with a lot of cancer patients. The Edward-Elmhurst Hospital is still taking the highest precautions for the patients and staff. Although they are not taking people's temperature before entering the building anymore, we still wore masks and social distance.

The nurse assigned to me was nurse Juliet and she was able to access my powerport without any problems. She's been one of my kind and compassionate nurses at the cancer center for many years now. My ovarian cancer level result is Cancer AG 125 (CA125) 3.6 U/mL. It is one of the lowest results I have had since 2011!

You may remember that before my ovarian cancer surgery in

2011, my CA125 was 4000 U/mL, after the surgery, it went down to 2000 U/mL, after my first few rounds of chemo it went down to lower than 20 U/mL. As of this date, it is 3.6 U/mL. The normal ovarian cancer level is less than 35.0 U/mL.

My follow-up appointment with Dr. Hantel was great! He is happy for me that I am doing very well. Despite my diagnosis of stage 4 aggressive metastatic ovarian cancer, my cancer responded very well to my chemotherapy treatments including all the side effects. I am now officially in remission! Thank GOD again and again!

Since my last cancer was in June 2016 my ovarian cancer level is steadily low and blood test results are good, I am now officially declared in remission for my stage 4 aggressive metastatic ovarian cancer and I am a six-time cancer survivor. I hope you learn something from my cancer story and will be strong enough to face your own battle with cancer.

Meanwhile, I will still be going for my regular three months ovarian cancer level, blood tests, other procedures, and follow-up with Dr. Hantel to prevent my cancer from coming back.

As you know my cancer is aggressive metastatic so there's a good chance that it will spread again to another part of my body. We just don't know when and which part of my body is next. When the cancer comes back, I will be treated the same way I was treated before. I give credit to these regular tests for catching all the cancers that I had and, for following everything Dr. Hantel advised me to do so.

There are times when I wonder if this cancer will ever leave my body. Will I have another cancer soon? Will it be the last one and I will be cancer free forever or will I die after the next one?

My oncologist told me with certainty that my cancer will come back, we just don't know when and which part of my body cancer will jump next to. Will I have the same energy to fight it one more time? After all, I just turned 68 years old last month. I am now 11 years older than when I had my first cancer.

Although technology and medications are now more advanced in treating cancer than years ago, I still think of these questions. I believe that all these questions are legitimate and reasonable for me to be thinking. Time will only tell!

CHAPTER 43: MY BROTHER RICO DIED UNEXPECTEDLY TODAY

I heard the sad and devastating news that my brother Rico died today. He was losing weight for a few months and consulted with different doctors in different hospitals. The doctors couldn't seem to find what was causing his weight loss. At this point, he was in and out of different hospitals with different doctors. When he was released from one of the hospitals, Rico had a bad fall that made him unconscious and his eyes were completely closed the whole time.

He was in the ICU of another hospital for a few days until the doctors declared that there was nothing else they could do to keep him alive. Since it was still COVID-19, the hospital was taking precautionary measures. A Catholic priest, a brother-in-law of one of my sister Tess' friends, Glo asked the priest to give Rico his last rites virtually.

Not even his wife was allowed in the hospital until the doctor said there was nothing else they could do for him. He was then transferred to a private room and his wife was allowed to be with him. According to his x-rays and death certificate, the bad fall caused a blood clot in his brain and broken ribs. Because he lost a lot of weight, he became so thin, his ribs went on top of each other.

He was so thin that he only weighed 47 lbs when he died. His eyes still closed, still unconscious, tears rolled down his face, and took his last breath with his wife, Ress beside him. Although he couldn't open his eyes, his tears were probably his way of saying goodbye to his wife.

He just turned 69 years old in August. He was a year older than me. He was a good and generous man that helped a lot of people financially (even the ones he didn't know personally), a respectful son, and a caring and loving husband and brother.

He really was my protector ever since we were children. He left behind his wife Ress of many years, three children Almira, Mella, and Mark, four grandchildren Cassie, Dylan, Annika, and Briana, and great-grandkids Cevi and Savi.

Just like my sister Tess, Rico was not able to go back and see his home one last time. They both died in two different hospitals and in two different cities. I find comfort in knowing that you are not suffering anymore. I miss and love you so much. Rest easy my brother! Until we all see each other again!

Now, two of my caring, loyal, and loving siblings died unexpectedly during my cancer journey. Tess and Rico were both healthy. They both did not show any signs of health problems. My brother Rico was only a year older than me and my sister Tess was three years older than me.

They died three years apart. I really miss both of them so much. We were always there for each other. They prayed very hard for me to survive cancer and now they are both gone! While I am still grieving for my sister Tess' death, I am also now grieving for my brother Rico's death!

None of us have the priviledge of knowing when our last day here on earth would be. So, tell your loved ones you love them and hug them a little tighter today!

CHAPTER 44: CONSULTATION WITH MY NEW PRIMARY DOCTOR

My doctor has a brand new modern office building located not too far away from where I live. It is a very nice big building compared to where they were. She told me that my glucose is high and she is concerned that I might have diabetes. So, I need to control my sugar intake by eating the right kind of food, fruits, vegetables, carbohydrates, and protein and staying away from pastries and desserts. I think for me this is the hardest part because I was born with a sweet tooth. I am not kidding. I always have to have dessert after dinner.

She also recommended that I learn how to eat 5 times a day instead of two times a day only. I feel like I will be eating the whole day, though. Portion control is a must as well. Of course, I know all these things. It is just hard to follow. Well, it's just another challenge in my journey but I will try my very best. Like I always do!

Also, I started using a blood monitor device on November 09,

2021 to see how food affects my blood sugar. It is twice a day before breakfast and two hours after a meal. It doesn't matter whether it is two hours after lunch or two hours after dinner. This means I have to prick my finger for a blood test for diabetes occasionally twice a day.

My doctor said that I have controlled diabetes. This means I do not need medication and insulin shots because my blood sugar is not that high yet but I can control my food intake and take my blood sugar occasionally by pricking my fingers. The normal blood sugar before breakfast is 130 mg/dl and the normal blood sugar two hours after lunch or two hours after dinner is 160 mg/dl.

I did this when I was pregnant with my daughter Megan in my third trimester because I couldn't eat regular food without throwing up. I started eating pies and cakes from Poppin Fresh, now Bakers Square but it elevated my blood sugar. By the time I had her my fingers were all swollen because I did the blood tests four times a day every day. But, oh, that was over 30 years ago! That was called gestational diabetes and it went away right after I had her.

I will try to do some light exercises. I just hope that my neuropathy in both hands and feet and my lymphedema in my right arm will cooperate. At least my cholesterol is under control. One out of two test results is not bad. I also had a flu shot while I was there. And, I will have another A1C Hemoglobin and lipid panel the first week of February 2022 and an appointment with Dr. Straczynski, MD after. That would be three months from now.

Wish me luck! I need all the luck that I can get!!!

CHAPTER 45: A LOOK BACK AT THE LAST DECADE

I never thought I was going to be celebrating another Thanksgiving dinner with my daughter Megan 10 years ago when we received that first awful ovarian cancer diagnosis. I am so thankful that my daughter Megan and I are healthy and happy, etc. This will be the last writing and the last chapter of my book. I think it is perfectly appropriate for me to end my story with a grateful and thankful heart on Thanksgiving Dinner 2021! Thank you so much, GOD!

I wrote this book to inspire and give hope to people who are still battling cancer, cancer survivors, friends, and family who are supporting their loved ones and caregivers.

I want them to know that I am living proof that being diagnosed with stage 4 cancer is not always a "death sentence". The treatments for cancer nowadays have improved a lot and are so advanced compared to even just 10 years ago. I don't really know the exact number but, I believe that there are millions of people like me who are surviving this awful disease. I'm eternally grateful to all the people who have discovered and invented treatments for cancer. Thank you very much! May GOD bless you all!

I am on a mission to help anyone going through cancer to keep hope alive! Stay strong, keep being positive, pray as you have never prayed before and live life fully one day at a time and keep on FIGHTING!

Listen to me, after so many years of dealing with my stage 4 aggressive metastatic ovarian cancer, surgeries, treatments, and its side effects, I am still alive after six cancers and I am still fighting every day. The only thing I have is to be positive (annoyingly positive at times).

I have strong faith in GOD (I now pray 5 rosaries a day). The first one thanking GOD for giving me another day to live. The second for my daughter, Megan. The third for my family Lynne, her family, friends and everyone I know and for others: (the living and the sick). The fourth is for my best bud Beth and her family. The fifth for my mom, dad, sister Tess, brother Rico and all the dead.

I have the utmost confidence and complete trust in my oncologist, Dr. Hantel, MD, and his medical team. I am truly blessed to have all of them on my side!

If I can just inspire one more additional patient to keep hope alive by telling my own cancer story, then I am glad that I have done my part! Please spread the word about my cancer journey. Thank you very much for reading my book! May GOD bless you all always!

Lastly, despite my chemo brain, neuropathy in both my hands and in both my feet (the reason why I have used a cane on long walks for over five years now), lymphedema in my right armpit and right arm, I still managed to write and finished this book in just five months. I am beyond thrilled and glad that I got it done! Where there's a will there's a way! I can honestly say that I endured cancer with great fortitude! This is the end of my cancer journey book. **My Pink Cane And Me!**

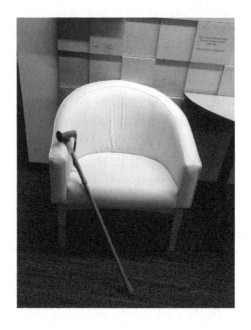

GLOSSARY:

A1C is a blood test for type 2 diabetes and prediabetes. It measures the average blood glucose or blood sugar level over the past 3 months.
https://www.medlineplus.gov

ANNUAL PHYSICAL is an exam of the head and neck, including tonsils, lymph nodes, and thyroid. An abdominal exam to check for any tenderness and liver size. It is also a check of your muscle strength, reflexes, and balance. Lab tests, such as a complete blood count (CBC), blood chemistry panel, and urinalysis.
https://www.avera.org Kevin Post, DO Chief Medical Officer, Avera Medical Group

BACK ON TRACK is a special physical exercise for cancer patients, cancer survivors, and caregivers offered and provided by well-qualified trained staff at Edward-Elmhurst Health Center.
https://www.eehealth.org/

BLOOD TESTS FOR CANCER samples collected for cancer blood tests are analyzed in a lab for signs of cancer. The samples may show cancer cells, proteins, or other substances made by cancer. Blood tests can also give your doctor an idea of how well your organs are functioning and if they have been affected by cancer.
https://www.mayoclinic.org By Mayo Clinic Staff

BLOOD TRANSFUSION is a routine medical procedure in which donated blood is provided to you through a narrow tube placed within a vein in your arm. This is a potentially life-

saving procedure that can help replace blood lost due to surgery or injury. A blood transfusion also can help if an illness prevents your body from making blood or some of your blood's components correctly.
https://www.mayoclinic.org

BONE DENSITY SCAN determines if you have osteoporosis. A disorder characterized by bones that are more fragile and more likely to break. The test uses x-rays to measure how many grams of calcium and other bone minerals are packed into a segment of bone. The bones that are most commonly tested are in the spine, hip, and sometimes the forearm.
https://www.mayoclinic.org

BRCA1 (Breast Cancer Gene 1) are genes that produce proteins that help repair damaged DNA. Everyone has two copies of each of these genes. One copy is inherited from each parent. BRCA1 and BRCA2 are sometimes called tumor suppressor genes because when they have certain changes, called harmful (or pathogenic) variants (or mutations), cancer can develop.
Source Credit: National Cancer Institute
https://www.cancer.gov

BRCA2 (Breast Cancer Gene 2) please see the definition above with BRCA1.
Source Credit: National Cancer Institute
https://www.cancer.gov

BREAST CANCER is a cancer that forms in the cells of the breasts. After skin cancer, breast cancer is the most common cancer diagnosed in women in the United States. Breast cancer can occur in both men and women, but it's far more common in women.
https://www.mayoclinic.org

BREAST NODULES are breast lumps. A breast lump is a mass that develops in your breast. While a breast lump can be a sign

of breast cancer, often it is not related to cancer. Eight out of 10 breast lumps are noncancerous.
https://my.clevelandclinic.org

CA 125 TEST measures the amount of the protein CA 125 (cancer antigen 125) in your blood. A CA 125 test may be used to monitor certain cancers during and after treatment. In some cases, a CA 125 test may be used to look for early signs of ovarian cancer in people with a very high risk of the disease.
https://www.mayoclinic.org

CALCIUM 500MG this medication is used to prevent or treat low blood calcium levels in people who don't get enough calcium from their diets. It may be used to treat conditions caused by low calcium levels such as bone loss (osteoporosis), weak bones (osteomalacia/rickets), and decreased activity of the parathyroid gland (hypoparathyroidism), and certain muscle diseases (latent tetany).
https://www.webmed.com

CHARITY FOUNDATION (also a charitable foundation) is a category of a nonprofit organization or charitable trust that typically provides funding and support for other charitable organizations through grants, but may also engage directly in charitable activities.
https://en.m.wikipedia.org

CHEMOTHERAPY is a drug treatment that uses powerful chemicals to kill fast-growing cells in your body. Chemotherapy is most often used to treat cancer since cancer cells grow and multiply much more quickly than most cells in the body. Many different chemotherapy drugs are available. Chemotherapy drugs can be used alone or in combination to treat a wide variety of cancers.
https://www.mayoclinic.org

CHOLESTEROL is a waxy, fat-like substance that's found in all

the cells in your body. Your body needs some cholesterol to make hormones, vitamin D, and substances that help you digest food. Your body makes all the cholesterol it needs.
https://medlineplus.gov

COBALT RADIATION the cobalt-60 system is designed to deliver radiation in the shape of a sphere. To cover irregularly shaped tumors, several of these radiation spheres are combined to best mimic the tumor's shape.
https://www.brainlab.org

COLONOSCOPY is an exam used to detect changes or abnormalities in the large intestine (colon) and rectum. During a colonoscopy, a long, flexible tube (colonoscope) is inserted into the rectum. A tiny video camera at the tip of the tube allows the doctor to view the inside of the entire colon.
https://www.mayoclinic.org

COVID-19 VACCINES are effective at helping protect against severe disease and death, including from variants of the virus that causes covid-19 currently circulating (e.g., Delta variant)
https://www.cdc.gov

CYBERKNIFE RADIATION the cyberknife system is a non-invasive treatment for cancerous and non-cancerous tumors and other conditions where radiation therapy is indicated. It is used to treat conditions throughout the body, including the prostate, lung, brain, spine, head and neck, liver, pancreas, and kidney, and can be an alternative to surgery or for patients who have inoperable or surgically complex tumors. Cyberknife treatments are typically performed in 1 to 5 sessions. The cyberknife system has more than two decades of clinical proof and has helped thousands of cancer patients.
https://cyberknife.com

ECZEMA (Atopic dermatitis) is a condition that makes your skin red and itchy. No cure has been found for atopic dermatitis.

But treatments and self-care measures can relieve itching and prevent new outbreaks. For example, it helps to avoid harsh soaps, moisturize your skin regularly and apply medicated creams or ointments.
https://www.mayoclinic.org

EXTRA STRENGTH TYLENOL CAPLETS for adult headache, muscle pain, and fever relief, 500mg acetaminophen
https://www.tylenol.com

FLU VACCINES influenza (flu) vaccines (often called "flu shots") are vaccines that protect against the four influenza viruses that research indicates are most common during the upcoming season. Most flu vaccines are "flu shots" given with a needle, usually in the arm, but there also is a nasal spray flu vaccine.
https://www.cdc.gov

HEPARIN FLUSH belongs to the family of drugs called anticoagulants. This is used to prevent blood from clotting or "stopping up" your intravenous (IV) line. Heparin, in the doses used to flush IV lines, should not normally keep your blood from clotting elsewhere in your body.
https://cookchildrens.org

HYSTERECTOMY an abdominal hysterectomy is a surgical procedure that removes your uterus through an incision in your lower abdomen. Your uterus or womb is where a baby grows if you're pregnant. A partial hysterectomy removes just the uterus, leaving the cervix intact. A total hysterectomy removes the uterus and the cervix.
https://www.mayoclinic.org

LIPID PANEL a complete cholesterol test also called a lipid panel or lipid profile is a blood test that can measure the amount of cholesterol and triglycerides in your blood. A cholesterol test can help determine your risk of the buildup of fatty deposits (plaques) in your arteries that can lead to narrowed or blocked arteries throughout your body (atherosclerosis).

https://www.mayoclinic.org

LOVASTATIN is used together with diet, weight loss, and exercise to reduce the risk of heart attack and stroke and to decrease the chance that heart surgery will be needed in people who have heart disease or who are at risk of developing heart disease.
https://medlineplus.gov

LOW DOSE 81MG ASPIRIN Taking aspirin every day may lower the risk of heart attack and stroke, but daily aspirin therapy isn't for everyone, is it right for you?
The answer depends on your age, overall health, history of heart disease, and risk of having a future heart attack or stroke.
https://www.mayoclinic.org

LUMPECTOMY is surgery to remove cancer or other abnormal tissue from your breast. During a lumpectomy procedure, the surgeon removes cancer or other abnormal tissue and a small amount of the healthy tissue that surrounds it. This ensures that all of the abnormal tissue is removed.
https://www.mayoclinic.org

LYMPHEDEMA refers to tissue swelling caused by an accumulation of protein-rich fluid that's usually drained through the body's lymphatic system. It most commonly affects the arms or legs, but can also occur in the chest wall, abdomen, neck, and genitals. Lymph nodes are an important part of your lymphatic system. Lymphedema can be caused by cancer treatments that remove or damage your lymph nodes. Any type of problem that blocks the drainage of lymph fluid can cause lymphedema.
https://www.mayoclinic.org

MAMMOGRAM is an x-ray picture of the breast. Doctors use a mammogram to look for early signs of breast cancer. Regular mammograms are the best test doctors have to find breast

cancer early, sometimes up to three years before it can be felt.
https://www.cdc.gov

METASTATIC OVARIAN CANCER The ovaries are almond-sized organs. One on each side of the uterus stores eggs and makes female hormones. When you have ovarian cancer, malignant cells begin to grow in the ovary. Cancer that starts in another part of your body can also spread or metastasize, to your ovaries, but that is not considered ovarian cancer.
https://www.webmd.com

MORPHINE tablets are used to relieve short-term (acute) or long-term (chronic) moderate to severe pain. The extended-release capsule and extended-release tablet are used to treat pain severe enough to require daily, around-the-clock, long-term opioid treatment and when other pain medicines did not work well enough or can not be tolerated. Morphine belongs to the group of medicines called narcotic analgesics (pain medicines). It acts on the central nervous system (CNS) to relieve pain.
https://www.mayoclinic.org

MRI (Magnetic Resonance Imaging) is a medical imaging technique that uses a magnetic field and computer-generated radio waves to create detailed images of the organs and tissues in your body. Most MRI machines are large, tube-shaped magnets. When you lie inside an MRI machine, the magnetic field temporarily realigns water molecules in your body. Radio waves cause these aligned atoms to produce faint signals, which are used to create cross-sectional MRI images - like slices in a loaf of bread.
https://www.mayoclinic.org

NEEDLE BIOPSY is a procedure to obtain a sample of cells from your body for laboratory testing. Common needle biopsy procedures include fine-needle aspiration and core needle biopsy. Needle biopsy may be used to take tissue or fluid samples from muscles, bones, and other organs such as the liver or lungs.

https://www.mayoclinic.org

NEUROPATHY peripheral neuropathy, a result of damage to the nerves located outside of the brain and spinal cord (peripheral nerves), often causes weakness, numbness, and pain, usually in the hands and feet. It can also affect other areas and body functions including digestion, urination, and circulation.
https://www.mayoclinic.org

OVARIAN CANCER LEVEL results of the CA 125 test are measured in units per milliliter (U/mL). The normal value is less than 46 U/mL. If your CA 125 level is higher than normal, you may have a benign condition, or the test result could mean that you have ovarian, endometrial, peritoneal, or fallopian tube cancer.
https://www.mayoclinic.org

OVARIAN CANCER SURGERY surgery is the main treatment for most ovarian cancers. How much surgery you have depends on how far your cancer has spread and your general health. For women of childbearing age who have certain kinds of tumors and whose cancer is in the early stage, it may be possible to treat the disease without removing both ovaries and the uterus.
https://www.cancer.org

PET SCAN (Positron Emission Tomography) for a PET scan, radioactive glucose (sugar) is given to look for cancer. Body cells take in different amounts of sugar, depending on how fast they are growing. Cancer cells, which grow quickly, are more likely to take up larger amounts of sugar than normal cells. A special camera is used to create a picture of areas of radioactivity in the body.
https://www.cancer.org

PNEUMONIA VACCINES helps prevent pneumococcal disease, which is any type of illness caused by Streptococcus pneumonia bacteria.

https://www.cdc.gov

POWERPORT DEVICE An implanted port (also known as a "port") is a flexible tube that's placed into a vein in your chest. It will make it easier for your healthcare team to: give you intravenous (IV, through a vein) medication. Give you IV fluids. Take blood samples. Give you medications continuously for several days. Sometimes medications must be given in a vein larger than the ones in your arms. The port lets your medication go into your bloodstream through a large vein near your heart.
https://www.mskcc.org

RADIATION THERAPY (also called radiotherapy) is a cancer treatment that uses high doses of radiation to kill cancer cells and shrink tumors. At low doses, radiation is used in x-rays to see inside your body, as with x-rays of your teeth or broken bones.
Source Credit: "Radiation Therapy to Treat Cancer was originally published by the National Cancer Institute".
https://www.cancer.gov

STAGE 0 BREAST CANCER describes non-invasive breast cancers, such as DCIS (ductal carcinoma in situ). In stage 0, there is no evidence of cancer cells or non-cancerous abnormal cells breaking out of the part of the breast in which they started, or getting through to or invading neighboring normal tissue.
https://www.breastcancer.org

STAGE 4 OVARIAN CANCER after a woman is diagnosed with ovarian cancer, doctors will try to figure out if it has spread, and if so, how far. This process is called staging. The stage of cancer describes how much cancer is in the body. It helps determine how serious the cancer is and how best to treat it. Doctors also use a cancer stage when talking about survival statistics. Ovarian cancer stages range from stage 1 (1) through IV (4). As a rule, the lower the number, the less cancer has spread. A higher number, such as stage IV, means cancer has spread more.

SENTINEL NODE BIOPSY (also called sentinel lymph node biopsy or SLNB) is a surgical procedure for people with cancer. During this procedure, the healthcare provider removes the sentinel nodes and sends them to a lab to test for cancer cells. Sentinel nodes are the first lymph nodes where cancer cells might spread from a tumor.

Lymph nodes are small organs that "filter" fluid in the body and help protect you from illness. The word "sentinel" means a guard or someone keeping watch.

SPRAINED ANKLE is an injury that occurs when you roll, twist, or turns your ankle in an awkward way. This can stretch or tear the tough bands of tissue (ligaments) that help hold your ankle bones together. Ligaments help stabilize joints, preventing excessive movement. A sprained ankle occurs when the ligaments are forced beyond their normal range of motion. Most sprained ankles involve injuries to the ligaments on the outer side of the ankle.

SPRAINED RIGHT WRIST a sprained wrist is an injury to its ligaments, the tough bands of fibrous tissue that connect bones to one another inside a joint. Although most people speak of the wrist as a single joint between forearm and hand, the wrist actually contains many joints that link 15 separate bones. The ligaments that connect these bones can be torn by any extreme twist, bend, or impact that suddenly forces the wrist into a position beyond its normal range of motion.

THYROID SCAN is a type of nuclear medicine imaging. The radioactive iodine uptake test (RAIU) is also known as thyroid uptake. It is a measurement of thyroid function but does not involve imaging.

https://www.radiologyinfo.org

ULTRASOUND SCAN in women, diagnostic ultrasound may be used to: look at a breast lump to see if it might be cancer. (The test may also be used to check for breast cancer in men, though this type of cancer is far more common in women).
https://medlineplus.gov

VITAMIN D is a nutrient your body needs for building and maintaining healthy bones. That's because your body can only absorb calcium, the primary component of bone when vitamin D is present. Vitamin D also regulates many other cellular functions in your body. Its anti-inflammatory, antioxidant, and neuroprotective properties support immune health, muscle function, and brain cell activity.
https://www.mayoclinic.org

WHY WEIGHT PROGRAM is a program for cancer patients and cancer survivors about eating healthy, etc. offered by Edward-Elmhurst Hospital Cancer Center
https://www.eehealth.org

Made in the USA
Las Vegas, NV
12 March 2023

68930348R00108